Dwayne Johnson

The Rock's Rise to Fame

By Ryan Nagelhout

Portions of this book originally appeared in
Dwayne Johnson by Sheila Wyborny.

LUCENT
PRESS

Published in 2019 by
Lucent Press, an Imprint of Greenhaven Publishing, LLC
353 3rd Avenue
Suite 255
New York, NY 10010

Designer: Deanna Paternostro
Editor: Vanessa Oswald

Library of Congress Cataloging-in-Publication Data

Names: Nagelhout, Ryan, author.
Title: Dwayne Johnson : The Rock's rise to fame / Ryan Nagelhout.
Description: New York : Lucent Press, [2019] | Series: People in the news
Identifiers: LCCN 2018000253 (print) | LCCN 2018001194 (ebook) | ISBN
  9781534563308 (eBook) | ISBN 9781534563292 (library bound book) | ISBN
  9781534563315 (pbk. book)
Subjects: LCSH: Johnson, Dwayne, 1972–Juvenile literature. | Motion picture
  actors and actresses–United States–Biography–Juvenile literatue. |
  Wrestlers–United States–Biography–Juvenile literature.
Classification: LCC PN2287.J5815 (ebook) | LCC PN2287.J5815 N34 2019 (print)
  | DDC 791.4302/8092 [B] –dc23
LC record available at https://lccn.loc.gov/2018000253

Printed in the United States of America

CPSIA compliance information: Batch #BS18KL: For further information contact Greenhaven Publishing LLC, New York,
New York at 1-844-317-7404.

Contents

Foreword

We live in a world where the latest news is always available and where it seems we have unlimited access to the lives of the people in the news. Entire television networks are devoted to news about politics, sports, and entertainment. Social media has allowed people to have an unprecedented level of interaction with celebrities. We have more information at our fingertips than ever before. However, how much do we really know about the people we see on television news programs, social media feeds, and magazine covers?

Despite the constant stream of news, the full stories behind the lives of some of the world's most newsworthy men and women are often unknown. Who was Katy Perry before she was a pop music phenomenon? What does LeBron James do when he's not playing basketball? What inspires Lin-Manuel Miranda?

This series aims to answer questions like these about some of the biggest names in pop culture, sports, politics, and technology. While the subjects of this series come from all walks of life and areas of expertise, they share a common magnetism that has made them all captivating figures in the public eye. They have shaped the world in some unique way, and—in many cases—they are poised to continue to shape the world for many years to come.

These biographies are not just a collection of basic facts. They tell compelling stories that show how each figure grew to become a powerful public personality. Each book aims to paint a complete, realistic picture of its subject—from the challenges they overcame to the controversies they caused. In doing so, each book reinforces the idea that even the most famous faces on the news are real people who are much more complex than we are often shown in brief video clips or sound bites. Readers are also reminded that there is even more to a person than what they present to the world through social media posts, press releases, and interviews. The whole story of a person's life can only be discovered by digging beneath the surface of their public persona, and that is what this series allows readers to do.

The books in this series are filled with enlightening quotes from speeches and interviews given by the subjects, as well as quotes and anecdotes from those who know their story best: family, friends, coaches, and colleagues. All quotes are noted to provide guidance for further research. Detailed lists of additional resources are also included, as are timelines, indexes, and unique photographs. These text features come together to enhance the reading experience and encourage readers to dive deeper into the stories of these influential men and women.

Fame can be fleeting, but the subjects featured in this series have real staying power. They have fundamentally impacted their respective fields and have achieved great success through hard work and true talent. They are men and women defined by their accomplishments, and they are often seen as role models for the next generation. They have left their mark on the world in a major way, and their stories are meant to inspire readers to leave their mark, too.

Introduction

Talent and Charisma

Dwayne "The Rock" Johnson's captivating personality makes it seem like he really, genuinely wants to be a friend to his fans. The incredible charisma with which Johnson operates in his life is unlike anything seen before in the celebrity world. In wrestling, sports, and even Hollywood, he has excelled and made a place for himself in three very different, sprawling fields. He can even sing, if he is in the mood to do so.

A football standout at the University of Miami, in Miami, Florida, he took up the family wrestling name to become the biggest wrestler in the world. Then, he left the wrestling world to take a role in a movie in which he barely spoke and somehow became the biggest, highest-paid movie star in the world. That is the basic story of Johnson, but how did he do it? He is supremely talented; however, it is much more than that. The fact is that The Rock has a personality so charismatic, so large, that he can effortlessly engulf all three worlds and make them his own.

His personality really does seem genuine. As Caity Weaver wrote in a *GQ* profile of Johnson in 2017, The Rock's charisma is immediate. He is perceptive, smart, and knows exactly how to relate to people in a way that is remarkably friendly. Weaver wrote,

Dwayne Johnson was a skilled football player before he became a wrestler.

If you are a child, good luck getting past Dwayne Johnson without a high five or some simulated roughhousing; if you're in a wheel-chair, prepare for a Beowulf-style epic poem about your deeds and bravery, composed extemporaneously [without planning], delivered to Johnson's Instagram audience of 85 million people; if you're dead, having shuffled off your mortal coil before you even got the chance to meet Dwayne Johnson, ... rest in peace knowing that Dwayne Johnson genuinely misses you. For Johnson, there are no strangers; there are simply best friends, and best friends he hasn't met yet.[1]

In a way, it is fitting that Johnson made his name in wrestling, the family business of sorts. Wrestling is a very unique world with its own set of rules and logic. It is a universe dominated by kayfabe, which is essentially acting like an alternate universe's reality is the truth. In wrestling, crazy storylines must be sold with all the seriousness of the real world. Fake injuries, fake marriages, and even fake deaths need to be treated as real. Whereas wrestling was once understood as real, most fans understand kayfabe and what is real and what is not. However, it takes huge personalities, great acting, and maybe a sly sense of humor to make wrestling feel real, and The Rock effortlessly managed to make all of it work in his favor.

Whether the "heel" (the "bad guy" in wrestling) or the "face" (the crowd favorite in wrestling), Dwayne Johnson has managed to turn wrestling fans in his favor at every turn. This often does come back to his personality.

Dwayne "The Rock" Johnson became a popular wrestler for the World Wrestling Federation (WWF), which was later renamed World Wrestling Entertainment (WWE).

Many people of all ages, demographics, and beliefs love him. Young women, elderly men, and children of all ages are charmed by his smile, his kindness, and his huge physique whether on Monday night wrestling programs on television or movies on the silver screen.

However, The Rock is more than just a winning smile and bulging muscles. In fact, the work he has put in to excel at all things makes him one of the most fascinating celebrities of the modern era. It is not easy being Dwayne "The Rock" Johnson, but it is a role the former defensive tackle for the Miami Hurricanes has created, and perfected, all on his own.

Chapter One

Born into the Ring Life

Dwayne Douglas Johnson was born on May 2, 1972, in Hayward, California. His father, Rocky Johnson, was a professional wrestler. His mother, Ata Johnson, was a relative of Samoan wrestling legends. It seems like Johnson was always destined to become a wrestler, because wrestling was certainly a business for his dad's family. Rocky Johnson was born Wayde Douglas Bowles, a black Canadian from Nova Scotia. He was part of the first black tag team to win the World Tag Team Championship in the World Wrestling Federation (WWF), today called World Wrestling Entertainment (WWE). Dwayne Johnson's mother, born Feagaimaleata Fitisemanu Maivia, also came from a wrestling family. Johnson's grandfather, "High Chief" Peter Maivia, wrestled and his grandmother, Lia Maivia, was a wrestling promoter who took over Polynesian Pacific Pro Wrestling after Peter died in 1982.

While working in California, Peter Maivia became acquainted with African Canadian wrestler Rocky "Soul Man" Johnson. Rocky Johnson drove trucks in Canada to support his wrestling as a teenager. He wrestled his first match in Toronto's Maple Leaf Gardens, but he soon moved to the West Coast of the United States to wrestle and even spar with

Dwayne Johnson is shown here with his parents, Ata and Rocky Johnson.

Johnson's father once sparred with legendary boxer George Foreman (shown here).

boxing legend George Foreman.

Johnson met Maivia's daughter Ata at the taping of one of the wrestling matches. The two soon began dating and fell in love. Maivia disapproved of the relationship and tried to break up the pair. Maivia objected to their relationship because Johnson was a wrestler, and since Maivia was a wrestler himself, he knew how hard a life his daughter would have if she married Johnson. At the time, although professional wrestling was popular entertainment, wrestlers did not make much money, and they had to move frequently. The couple would not be discouraged, though. Since the family objected so strongly to their intended marriage, Ata and Rocky eloped, which means they ran away to get married without their parents' permission. After they went against her father's wishes, the young couple was estranged from Ata's family for nearly a year. The relationship improved when their son, Dwayne, was born. In fact, Johnson was finally accepted as a member of the Maivia wrestling family.

Dwayne was Rocky and Ata Johnson's first and only child. Some of his first toys were his father's championship belts, and at five years old, he would often sit ringside with his mother while his father wrestled. He later spoke of his early exposure to the world of wrestling: "I grew up in the business, was kept close to the business, and never sheltered from it."[2]

Johnson was a very active child and prone to mischief. As a small child, he would crawl out of his crib at night to play instead of going to sleep. At the armories and stadiums where his father wrestled, Johnson would slip away from his mother and go exploring. Not even the family pet escaped his mischief. By the time Dwayne started school, he was using his dog to practice wrestling moves. At this point in his life, though, his parents were sure wrestling was just a game to him, another way to play and use up some of his extra energy. At least they hoped so.

The wrestling business was hard on families. Some stayed behind while the wrestler traveled the United States to different wrestling territories and matches. However, Rocky Johnson did not want to be separated from his family. He took them with him when he moved from territory to territory, which meant that they moved frequently.

Always the New Kid

Moving around a lot meant that Johnson was generally the new kid on the block, and after he was old enough to go to school, the new kid in class. As he grew older and larger, other boys often picked fights with him so they could prove how tough they were. Johnson typically did not start the fights, but he did not back away from them, either. Since he was generally the largest kid on the playground, he won the fights,

The Wrestling World

Kayfabe in the wrestling world means that viewers are experiencing part entertainment and part sport. The feuds and friction between wrestlers consist of scripted storylines, called angles, and the matches themselves have been carefully planned and choreographed. Many wrestlers who appear to be mortal enemies in the ring are, in fact, actually good friends. After hurling one another around the ring and slinging insults and threats, they may go out to dinner together.

However, the risk of injury is quite real. Wrestlers are carefully trained athletes, and, like any other athletes, despite careful preparations, they are sometimes injured. Dislocated shoulders, torn ligaments, concussions, and other injuries which may require surgery or physical therapy can take them away from their sport for anywhere from a few days to several months. Johnson has suffered many injuries during his time in the ring, and he has missed time in the acting and wrestling world recovering from these injuries.

and sometimes the other boys got hurt. When this happened, Johnson was labeled a bully, even when he was defending himself. One of these fights was not even a real fight—it was actually a demonstration. One of Johnson's friends had asked Johnson to show him some of the wrestling moves he had learned from his father. During the demonstration the boy was injured. Johnson felt bad about hurting his friend and had not meant to injure him. However, Johnson was still suspended from school for fighting, which got him into trouble with his mother. She was the parent in charge of handing out the discipline.

Despite the frequent moves and getting into trouble

for fighting, Johnson was a good student and made good grades. His parents wanted their son to get a good education so he could have a better life. They made sure he did not miss school, studied for his tests, and kept up with his homework, no matter how much they moved. With good grades, they knew that their son would be able to get into college and have a career that would allow him the opportunity to put down roots somewhere and have a normal home life.

One of the family's moves took them to Hawai'i, where Johnson was able to spend some time with his grandparents. Now eight years old, Johnson was old enough to understand what an important man his grandfather was and that he was respected both inside and outside of the wrestling community. However, his time with his grandfather would be brief. Maivia had worked hard to promote his wrestling territory but had neglected his own health. He refused to go to the doctor when he had obvious warning signs that his health and his life were in jeopardy. By the time Maivia did go to the doctor, it was too late. Johnson's grandfather, wrestling legend "High Chief" Peter Maivia, died from cancer on June 12, 1982. His grandfather's memorial service in Honolulu, Hawai'i, attended by thousands of fans and friends, reinforced what Johnson already knew—that his grandfather had been an important and greatly respected man.

Focusing on Football

Johnson returned to the mainland a few years after his grandfather's death, moving this time to Pennsylvania. While living in Pennsylvania, he developed a serious interest in football. He worked hard to become a good football player and to keep up with his studies.

Through hard work and using his size, Johnson became one of the top high school football players in the state of Pennsylvania. During his senior year, a number of colleges were scouting him. By the time he graduated from high school, he had been approached by a number of colleges

The Samoan Culture

Most fans know that Johnson's father is African Canadian and his mother is Samoan. Johnson has always taken pride in the heritage of each of his parents. However, many people know little about the Samoan culture.

Samoa is a group of 10 islands in the South Pacific, about 2,600 miles (4,184.3 km) southwest of Hawai'i. Said to be Polynesia's oldest culture, Samoans have occupied these islands for more than 3,000 years. Samoa means "sacred Earth." To the Samoan people, this island group is a sacred place, and they protect and cherish it.

Their system of government is called fa'amatai. The matai, or chief, governs the aiga, or extended family. The members of the aiga respect their chief and revere their elders. They are generous toward one another and take the same care of the children of other adults in their group as they do their own. They believe their

with offers of football scholarships. He later recalled that exciting time:

It's amazing what a simple letter can do to a kid's ego. You walk to the mailbox and there's an envelope with Penn State or Notre Dame stamped in the upper left-hand corner, and your heart just about does a somersault. Then the phone starts ringing ... day and night. And then the assistant coaches begin showing up, knocking at your front door after dinner or visiting you at school. It's extraordinarily flattering, and it can really go to your head if you're not careful.[3]

extended families should work together and be mutually supportive for the common good.

Samoans are known for their handcrafted products, such as kava bowls. These are round wooden bowls of a variety of sizes with stubby legs on the bottom. Another Samoan craft is called siapo. Siapo are pictures or patterns painted on paper mulberry bark that has been hammered into sheets.

Samoan crafts, traditional music and dance, and government have been handed down through generations. The Samoans are a proud people who respect and honor the culture handed down by their ancestors and work diligently to keep it alive.

In 2016, Johnson starred in the animated Disney movie *Moana*, playing the character of Maui, a shapeshifting demigod. The character, who has a striking resemblance to Johnson's grandfather, is partly inspired by his grandfather "High Chief" Peter Maivia, Johnson said. Johnson's cultural heritage is reflected in the movie, especially because the setting of the film is the Polynesian islands, which is where his Samoan ancestors are from.

Johnson considered all the offers and opportunities. Ultimately, he settled on the University of Miami because he respected their recruiting methods. They did not offer him anything under the table, such as cars or money. They just offered him the opportunity to go to college and play football.

Early Struggles in College

Johnson arrived on campus at the University of Miami in 1990, ready to begin football practice. There, he experienced a large dose of culture shock. First, Johnson had never been away from his family and on his own. Second, at the

Johnson is shown here in the white jersey playing a game for the University of Miami.

University of Miami, he was not the largest football player or as big a star as he had been in high school. Many of the other players were as large as Johnson, and many of them could play football just as well as he could. Some were simply a lot better.

Johnson had plenty of work ahead of him during the summer training program if he expected to see time on the field as a freshman. He was willing to work hard and do whatever he had to do to get that opportunity. Finally, toward the end of summer football practice with the first game practically in sight, Johnson was tackled from behind and taken to the ground during a practice session. He had been tackled many times over the summer, but this time something went wrong.

The U

Johnson was given an athletic scholarship to the University of Miami, where he played defensive line for the Miami Hurricanes from 1991 to 1994. The team was very successful during his time there, winning the Big East Championship three times and tying for it once. The U, as the school is called, has a legendary football program, winning five national titles as of 2018. It regularly recruits top tier players and is known for its fierce play on defense and exciting style on the field. Johnson fit right in at Miami, a school known for its swagger and toughness.

His shoulder was badly injured. The trainers could see right away that it had popped from its socket. Johnson was in tremendous pain as he was rushed to the hospital by ambulance. X-rays and magnetic resonance imaging (MRI) confirmed a separated shoulder as well as a number of torn ligaments. The injuries required surgery and weeks of physical therapy. Johnson was not out for a few games; he was out for the entire season.

Seriously depressed, Johnson began skipping classes. His grades fell so low that by the end of the semester he was placed on academic probation. Although he had been a good student throughout school, his grade average had slipped to 0.7 out of a possible 4.0. This was almost as hard to take as the tackle that had knocked him out of the season.

"In that moment, I felt about as worthless as I had ever felt in my life," Johnson said. "I had let my parents down, I had let my teammates and coaches down, and I had let myself down."[4]

Instead of giving up and going home, though, Johnson fought through his disappointment and accepted the terms of his probation. He had to carry a paper around to all of his classes and have his professors sign it. This piece of paper was his admission slip to football practice. Without it, he could not attend practice. After months of mandatory tutoring and study sessions, Johnson had improved his grades enough to get off of probation and back on the team.

Bouncing Back

Johnson was happy to be back on the team, and he intended to keep up his grades and work hard in practice sessions to stay there. He also had another especially good experience during this time. While studying at the University of Miami, he met his future wife, Dany Garcia, who was also a student at the college. Although he was 18 and just starting college, and she was 21 and nearly finished with college, they became a couple.

The University of Miami's football team won the Orange Bowl on January 2, 1992, and Johnson continued to play through his next two years. However, he was replaced as a starter by future Pro Football Hall of Famer Warren Sapp, and during Johnson's senior year, he suffered another injury, rupturing two disks in his lower back. He was told to take two weeks off from football but was back on the field in

Future Pro Football Hall of Famer Warren Sapp (shown here) replaced Johnson as a starter in college.

The CFL and NFL: Same Sport, Different Rules

Johnson encountered a few surprises during his brief stint with the Canadian Football League (CFL). One thing a Canadian player might have told him is that football actually came to the United States from Canada about 130 years ago. Once in America, the size of the field changed, and the rules were modified.

Actually, when written on paper, all the differences in the rules could cover several pages. The first obvious difference is that U.S. football is played on a smaller field. This leads to one of the most basic differences—the number of players allowed on the field during a play. In Canada it is 12 players. In the United States, the number is 11. One of the most notable differences, though, is in salaries of professional football players. In Canada, the salaries range from about $35,000 for rookies to $250,000 for starting quarterbacks, whereas in the United States, salaries for the top NFL players can reach into the millions.

just a few days. It was his senior year, and if he hoped to be drafted by the National Football League (NFL), he had to be seen on the field. Despite his best efforts, though, Johnson was passed over by NFL teams.

He was drafted by the Calgary Stampeders, a team in the Canadian Football League (CFL). Although he knew the pay would be very low, he needed a job. Arriving in Calgary, Canada, he learned the pay would be even lower than he originally thought. He would be only a practice player with a weekly paycheck of $250. To get by, Johnson and three other players rented a dingy apartment, which they furnished with whatever useful items they could pull from dumpsters. To eat, Johnson went to practice sessions and meetings he did not have to attend—he knew that food would be served there.

Getting Cut

On his lowest day, Johnson was called into the team office. He was cut as a practice player and was replaced by a player who had just been cut from the NFL. Johnson was stunned. As bad as things had been, at least he had been earning a paycheck. At 23, he felt like a washed-up has-been. With no hope of a position with another team in Canada or the United States, or any other job prospects, all he could think to do was fly back to Miami, to Dany.

After his experiences in Canada, Johnson's self-esteem was at an all-time low. "My goal was to make it in the NFL. I played with a lot of great players in college who went on to have illustrious, incredible careers and in the end it just didn't happen for me."[5]

Dany said she would stand with him no matter what. Finally, he made his decision: He would join the family business and attempt to make it as a wrestler.

Johnson knew his father would not like his decision. In fact, it would probably be easier to be slammed into the ground by a 275-pound (125 kg) defensive tackle than to tell his father he wanted to become a professional wrestler. However, Johnson made the phone call. First, he asked his father to drive down from Tampa, Florida, where Johnson's parents were then living, and pick him up at Dany's apartment. Next, he told him that he wanted to become a professional wrestler and furthermore, wanted his father to be the one to train him. Without a second's hesitation, Rocky Johnson got into his truck and made the exhausting 560-mile (901.23 km) round trip.

The issue of his son becoming a professional wrestler, though, was another matter. He intended to do everything he could to talk Dwayne out of what he thought was a bad decision. Rocky Johnson pulled no punches. He hit his son with every argument he had. All the way to Tampa, Johnson and his

Becoming a professional football player had been Johnson's dream.

father discussed his situation. His father wanted him to be patient, wait for the next season, and give football another chance. After all, why would any-one spend four years in college just to become a wrestler and be slammed around a ring for the next 30 or so years?

Making a Plan

After they arrived in Tampa, many heated discussions took place during the next week as Johnson went ahead and mapped out his plans. First, he needed a job. He found one as a personal fitness trainer at a local health club. The job did not pay very well, but Johnson did not need a lot of money. What he did need was access to workout equipment, which he was free to use whenever he did not have clients or the club was not busy. Also, since the job was part-time, he had plenty of time to train to be a wrestler.

Although Johnson's father was still reluctant to see his son go into the family business, if it was going to happen, then he was going to be the one to begin his son's training. From the beginning they maintained a tough training schedule.

Johnson said, "My dad rose to the occasion … He said, 'I'll train you.' And it wound up being one of the greatest chapters in my life."[6]

Up before daylight, the two worked together for several hours before Johnson drove to the health club to work with his clients. When he was finished with his clients for the day, Johnson was back in the practice ring, either with his father or one of his father's friends, working on the basic moves, over and over again, until Johnson's father was satisfied that his son had the moves down just right.

Since Johnson had grown up around wrestling, he was already familiar with the vocabulary of the ring and what the names of the moves meant. When his father told him to do a certain move, he could immediately go into the correct position. For instance, one of the more common wrestling moves is called a headlock. To do a headlock, one wrestler holds their opponent's head with their arm. The body slam is a move where a wrestler picks up their opponent and slams them to the floor. Another move, and one of the most dangerous, is called the pile driver. To do this, the wrestler lifts their opponent upside down and appears to slam their opponent's head into the floor of the ring. If not done properly, this move can cause serious injury. Johnson understood how important it was for wrestlers to perfect every move, both to avoid injury and to put on a good show. He also wanted to perform well when it came time for his professional audition.

Training to become a wrestler was even more intense than college football training camp. As he practiced his moves, he also worked on developing what he hoped would someday become his signature moves, moves that would be identified with him. One of these moves is called the kip-up. To perform this move, the wrestler must jump straight to his feet from lying flat on the ground. He does not use his hands or even roll his body over. The move requires extreme physical agility and strength. Johnson practiced this physically demanding move many times each day. He also wanted to be able to land on his feet when his opponents gave him a back-drop, which is

Johnson became known as "The Rock" after his football career ended.

tossing one's opponent into the air over the wrestler's back when the opponent repels off of the ropes. Johnson was not satisfied until he thought he had perfected these moves.

Trying It Out

After months of grueling work, Rocky Johnson decided his son was ready to be evaluated by an objective professional, so he called on his old friend, the former wrestling legend Pat Patterson. Not only was Patterson a friend of Rocky Johnson, he had also wrestled against his grandfather, Peter Maivia. Patterson agreed to watch Dwayne work out in the ring to see if he thought Dwayne had potential as a professional wrestler. Although it was easier for Dwayne to secure such a meeting, since his family had been in the wrestling business for two generations, he knew he would not get a second chance to make a first impression. He understood how important this first impression would be to his future.

Johnson had learned his basic moves. He had also worked on

timing and the acting part of professional wrestling. In wrestling, acting is called "selling." In the case of a wrestling match, a good sell would be convincing the spectators that every slam against the mat is agonizing and every time the opponent has the wrestler's head in a headlock, he is about to get his neck broken. Dany was in Tampa for the weekend and attended this workout. She did not know about selling, though, and when she saw her boyfriend being hurt, or so she thought, she broke down in tears.

At the end of the session, Johnson asked Patterson if he thought he was any good in the ring. Patterson's answer was very encouraging. He assured Johnson that he had the makings of a professional wrestler, and he told Johnson that he should continue training. That was all Johnson needed to hear. If Patterson thought he had what it took to be a professional wrestler, then he would keep working toward that all-important first match.

Pat Patterson (shown here on the left) was a legendary wrestler who agreed to see if Johnson had a chance at becoming a professional wrestler.

The wait was not as long as Johnson might have expected, though. The very next week, Patterson called Johnson to tell him he was booking him on a flight to Corpus Christi, Texas, for a tryout match. Johnson was happy and excited. He called Dany in Miami and told her the news. A new chapter in his life was about to begin.

Chapter Two

Becoming
a Celebrity Wrestler

In March 1996, Johnson boarded the plane for Corpus Christi and his first tryout with the WWF. Every wrestler must come up with their own ring name. For some, it reflects a gimmick or specific angle they bring to their character. However, Johnson had a unique problem: already a member of a wrestling family, should he adopt his father's or grandfather's persona or try to go it alone?

Johnson decided he did not want to use his father's or his grandfather's names. He did not want anyone to think that he had made it to the ring riding on their careers, so, since he could not think of a professional name at that time, he decided he would take his first step into the profession under his own name, Dwayne Johnson. His first professional wrestling opponent was Steve Lombardi, known as the "Brooklyn Brawler." A wrestler since the 1980s, Lombardi was one of the best-known jobbers in the business. In wrestling, a jobber is a professional loser. If a jobber is part of a match, it is pretty certain that his opponent will win. Johnson was excited but also nervous. After all, his future as a professional wrestler hung on this tryout. However, he had worked hard and trained well. He felt he was ready.

The match was what is known in the wrestling business as

a "dark match." This means that the match was not scheduled to appear on television. Despite this, though, several important people were among the spectators. One of them was Vince McMahon, the owner of the WWF. Not surprisingly, Johnson won his first match. Even though the win was a foregone conclusion, it was Johnson's performance and the way he handled himself in the ring that impressed McMahon and the other WWF officials present.

Vince McMahon (shown here) was one of the first people to see Johnson wrestle and to decide if he had a future in the business.

The second half of his tryout occurred on the next night. This time his opponent was Chris Candido. Before the match, Johnson and Candido spent some time planning what they would do in the ring, almost like planning a stunt scene for a movie. This was important if they were going to give a good show without anyone being hurt. However, this time Johnson lost. Johnson flew home to Tampa both anxious and encouraged. He had done a good job, put on a good show and, probably the best part of the tryout, McMahon had seen what the young wrestler could do in the ring. Johnson knew that if McMahon had liked the match, he would probably be back in the ring soon,

The Impact of
Vince McMahon

The chairman of the board of the WWE and a major shareholder, Vince McMahon is a wrestling promoter and film producer. In the world of professional wrestling, McMahon has been involved in a number of wrestling storylines, or angles. He also sometimes gets into the ring himself.

A second-generation wrestling promoter, McMahon began his association with the wrestling business through the WWF, a promotion started by his father Vincent J. McMahon. He promoted the first WrestleMania at Madison Square Garden in March 1985. In addition to wrestlers at this event, McMahon hired well-known pianist Liberace, The Rockettes, and pop singer Cyndi Lauper to perform. He risked most of his personal finances on the event, and it paid off. This event led to what has been called the Second Golden Age of Wrestling.

In the 1990s, McMahon became heavily involved in WWF storylines as Mr. McMahon, the egotistical heel boss of the WWF, later the WWE. He was involved in feud storylines with Steve Austin, Bret Hart, and

this time for keeps. In the meantime, he worked, trained, and waited. The hardest part was the waiting.

Signing Up

A few days after returning to Tampa, Johnson got his answer: He was in. He received his first wrestling contract. In the beginning, his paychecks would not be much, but it was a start, and he was delighted to have the opportunity. The

Vince McMahon sometimes played a part in the spectacle he created. Bret "The Hitman" Hart (shown here) is a famous wrestler who was part of a staged feud with McMahon.

Mankind, among others. In fact, no storyline is too extreme for McMahon. In June 2007, he was supposedly blown up in a limousine. McMahon later assured CNBC that he was not actually dead. His "hands on" approach to the WWE has been instrumental in making it the only remaining major professional wrestling promotion in the United States.

contract was basic; a guarantee of $150 per match, which Johnson was happy to get after being so broke.

First, he would go to Memphis, Tennessee, the home of the United States Wrestling Alliance (USWA). This was something like a professional hockey or baseball team's farm team (a farm team is a minor division that provides players as needed to major divisions). However, the USWA had its own stars. Though not a large wrestling promotion, or territory, the USWA was home to Jerry "The King" Lawler and Jeff Jarrett, both well-known wrestlers. Johnson knew the WWF people kept regular tabs on all the USWA wrestlers. They received regular reports on the wrestlers and films of their matches. From the Memphis group, they would choose which wrestlers would move up to the WWF.

The Big Move

Jerry "The King" Lawler is a wrestling legend who was part of the United States Wrestling Alliance when Johnson joined.

In May, just two months after his first tryout match, Johnson bought a used SUV, loaded it with his belongings, and began the 850-mile (1,368 km) drive to Memphis. On the long trip, Johnson had plenty of time to think about his future as a wrestler. Of course it would be hard being farther away from Dany, and making any plans for their future together had to be on hold for a while. He also needed to think of a name to use in the ring and think about what type of a character he would be. All he was sure of was that he did not want to be gimmicky, with masks and flashy costumes. As he left Tampa, he did not have the answers to any of his questions. He was still determined, though, that he would not take advantage of his father's or his grandfather's name. He wanted his own ring name, something that sounded a little flashy, but also strong—a name people could remember. He settled on "Flex" for the strength part and "Kavana" as a tribute to his Samoan heritage.

Looking back on it, he realized "Flex Kavana" was not really a great name, but it was the best he could do. "When I said the name aloud—Flex Kavana—it sounded like a name I could live with," Johnson said. "It had a nice marketable ring to it. One thing was for sure: Nobody else had ever called themselves Flex Kavana. For better or worse, it was my name."[7]

The USWA

The United States Wrestling Alliance (USWA) was born in Memphis in 1989. It was formed by the merging of Fritz Von Erich's World Class Championship Wrestling and Jerry Jarrett's Continental Wrestling Association. They were attempting to create a third national wrestling promotion. Although it was not actually a farm team and in fact had a number of its own stars, such as Jerry "The King" Lawler, Junkyard Dog, Brian Christopher, and Dwayne Johnson (known during this time as Flex Kavana), it became a training ground for up-and-coming young wrestlers. By October 1996, though, the USWA had run its course. It disbanded after being sold to XL Sports, a group based in Cleveland, Ohio. The last USWA event, at the Big One Flea Market Pavilion, drew only 372 fans, taking in less than $2,000.

Paying His Dues

Johnson said he was willing to do whatever it took to make it as a wrestler. However, the first news that greeted Johnson when he arrived in Memphis was a disappointment. He would not be paid $150 a match as he had first thought. As a trainee, he would be paid only $40 a night. Rather than give up, he drove through the bleaker parts of Memphis until he found an elderly couple who were willing to rent a room to him.

One day after arriving in Memphis, Johnson had his first wrestling event, a tag team match. As Flex Kavana, he entered the ring with a wrestler named Brian Christopher. They went against USWA star Jerry "The King" Lawler and his partner, Bill Dundee. The match became little more than a brawl, or a "schmozz" in wrestling language, but Johnson earned his first $40.

Sometimes Johnson fought in professional wrestling rings, but more often than not, he fought his matches in wobbly, makeshift rings temporarily rigged on fairgrounds, in asphalt parking lots, and even in barns. Other obstacles included times when the spectators were more dangerous than his opponents. Occasionally, spectators became so drunk and rowdy that they threw things at the wrestlers, causing cuts and bruises.

There were rewards, though. For example, on June 17, 1996, just a month after moving to Memphis, Johnson, as Flex Kavana, and his then–tag team partner Buzz Sawyer won the USWA Tag Team title. His time in Tennessee also involved putting a lot of miles on his used SUV. He later described a normal Saturday's work schedule: "On Saturdays I worked a live TV show in Memphis in the morning, then drove to Nashville for a show at the Nashville Fairgrounds that evening. After that show I'd climb in my truck and drive back to Memphis. I almost never stayed overnight because I couldn't afford a hotel."[8]

On Saturdays alone, Johnson's round-trip drive was 430 miles (692 km). Aside from his long drive on Saturdays, he drove to other matches outside of Memphis and put an average of 1,700 miles (2,736 km) on his SUV every week. In a month's time, that added up to nearly 7,000 miles (11,265 km) on a vehicle that was already secondhand when he bought it. Not only was he adding wear-and-tear to his vehicle, he was also spending a lot of his hard-earned money on gasoline.

Due to his low pay and the amount of money he had to spend on transportation, life in Memphis was a real challenge for the young wrestler. When it came to making ends meet, Johnson was cutting it pretty close. To make more money,

Owen Hart (shown here) was a wrestler Johnson grappled with early on in his career who later became a close friend.

he sometimes sold his own autographed photographs after matches. He had kept up this exhausting pace for nearly six months when he received a call from the WWF: He was being sent to Columbus, Ohio, for another two-night tryout match.

He won the first night's match against David Haskins. Johnson's opponent the second night was the well-known wrestler Owen Hart. Hart was known for his sense of humor and his practical jokes, such as the false arm cast he wore during their match. He did not admit the cast was a fake until they were already working in the ring. Once Johnson understood he had been duped, they put on a good show. Although Hart won this match, he told McMahon that he thought Johnson was at least as good if not better than many of the wrestlers already working in the WWF. Over the years, the two would become friends, but at that particular moment, Johnson was basking in the praise of one of his favorite wrestlers, and it felt good.

To Better Things

Johnson was a happy man when he returned to Memphis. Hart's opinion meant a lot to him. He watched videotapes of the best wrestlers in the WWF and worked harder than ever to correct any of his weak areas. After his match with Hart, Johnson was signed for a few more matches. Finally, in October 1996, he was offered his first contract with the WWF. While he was grateful for all that he had learned in Memphis, he was more than ready to get started on the next step in his wrestling career, and he moved to Stamford, Connecticut, where the WWF headquarters were located. As Memphis disappeared behind him, so did the ring name Flex Kavana. Johnson was headed for Connecticut and his future with the WWF.

Making the Big Time

Johnson was put through his paces in Stamford, training for many hours every day by working on different moves and routines. Even the moves he thought he knew well he learned to do better. While working to perfect his moves and routines, Johnson still needed to settle the matter of his ring name. The WWF officials suggested the name Rocky Maivia. At first, Johnson resisted. He had not changed his mind about what kind of wrestler he wanted to be. He did not want costumes, body paint, or other gimmicks, and he did not want anyone to think that he had used his father's and his grandfather's careers to get him into the WWF. However, the officials convinced him that by using parts of his father's and grandfather's names, he was not capitalizing on their careers; he was honoring them. Once it was explained to him that way, and after discussing it with Dany and his family, Johnson decided he could use the name with a clear conscience. After all, he had a great deal of respect for both his father and his late grandfather.

Finally, on November 17, 1996, the newly named Rocky Maivia made his official WWF debut in the WWF Survivor Series at Madison Square Garden in New York City. This was by far the most important day in Johnson's life. The Garden was far different from any other place he had wrestled. He was awed by the sheer size of the place. Johnson had been used to much smaller crowds. The matches he fought in makeshift rings in parking lots drew dozens to maybe as much as a

The Garden

Madison Square Garden is one of the most famous sports and entertainment arenas in the United States. Called "the Garden" by local New Yorkers, the current Madison Square Garden, the fourth by the same name, was built in 1968 above a working railroad line. The name Madison Square Garden has two sources. One is the location of the first Garden, at East 26th Street and Madison Avenue. The other is Madison Square Park, a beautiful 19-century garden and park located in New York City.

The current Garden underwent a $200 million renovation in 1991 and another $1 billion renovation from 2011 to 2013. Today, it is the home of the New York Rangers hockey team, as well as the New York Knicks and the New York Liberty basketball teams. It was also where the WWE held several WrestleMania and SummerSlam events. In addition to sports, the Garden also hosts many popular music events and graduation ceremonies. It was also the site where the Ringling Bros. and Barnum & Bailey Circus was staged when it came to New York City.

couple hundred wrestling fans. The smaller arenas held several hundred. Madison Square Garden had seating for up to 20,000 wrestling fans.

In addition to being a huge facility, the Garden was careful about security. No behavior problems with unruly fans were tolerated at Madison Square Garden. Rules concerning fan conduct were in writing. Fans were to be respectful to those around them. They could not interfere with the events in any way. Offensive language, fighting, and throwing objects were not tolerated. Whether or not they drank alcohol, the fans were responsible for their own behavior. This meant that all the wrestlers had to worry about were their opponents, not the behavior of the spectators.

The Garden has an impressive history. The current Garden, opened in 1968, four years before Johnson was born, was actually the fourth Madison Square Garden. The first one opened in 1879. Since its creation, the Garden has had the reputation of hosting world-class sporting events and the best of entertainment. When Dwayne Johnson, also known as Rocky Maivia, stepped into the ring at Madison Square Garden that November day, he was not just performing in his first WWF event, he was becoming part of the history of the Garden.

Learning to Grapple

For this match, eight wrestlers, four to a team, would fight until all the members of one team had been pinned. Rocky Maivia was teamed with Jake Roberts, Marc Mero, and Barry Windham. Their opponents were Jerry Lawler, Crush, Goldust, and WWF Intercontinental Champion Hunter Hearst Helmsley, later known as Triple H. In addition to the huge crowd in the Garden, the event was also televised via pay-per-view. The spectators in the crowd and the viewers at home had one thing in common: Few, if any of them, had heard of Dwayne Johnson, and no one had ever heard of Rocky Maivia. Since his new persona was unknown, when Rocky Maivia entered the WWF ring that first time, the fan response was lukewarm, at best.

First, Roberts took down Lawler, then Goldust pinned Windham. When Mero pinned Helmsley and Crush pinned Roberts, Maivia was one of the two remaining members still on his feet. First, Maivia pinned Crush, then he took down Goldust. Half an hour after entering the ring, Rocky Maivia had pinned his team's last opponent to the mat, and his team had won the match. It had been an impressive debut for Rocky Maivia, and Johnson knew that every wrestling fan, at home or in the Garden, who had seen the match would remember

his new ring name. This win began the process of building his reputation as a professional wrestler. Johnson knew he was still very much in a learning process, though, and his matches were pretty much warm-ups for the headlining bouts. At this point in his career, his job was to smile at the fans and keep his mouth shut. He was concentrating on his performance as a wrestler, not on developing a personality to support his ring name.

Triple H (shown here) was one of Johnson's first WWF opponents at Madison Square Garden.

First Championship

Rocky Maivia's first major success occurred just a few months after that first match in Madison Square Garden. On February 13, 1997, with just three months of experience as a WWF wrestler, he won the Intercontinental Championship by defeating Triple H. This win made Johnson the youngest Intercontinental Champion in the history of the WWF. He was three months short of his 25th birthday. Johnson was happy with the direction his career was moving. He was appearing in many matches throughout the country, winning an impressive number of these matches and starting to become a household name as a professional wrestler.

When it came to his ring character, however, something was missing from the polite, smiling Rocky Maivia. At the time, Johnson thought the problem was that he had taken this title so early in his career that the fans simply were not buying it, as though they thought the championship had come to him too easily. However, the fans had no way of knowing about all the work he had done to get ready for his first championship match. Even though the "win" had already been scripted, professional matches have to be well rehearsed and the wrestlers have to be in top physical form so they will not be injured. Fans did not like Maivia, though. Whatever the reason, Rocky Maivia was not getting the kind of fan response Dwayne Johnson wanted.

Johnson was a very attractive young man with a dazzling smile and a pleasant personality. These were the same qualities he brought into the ring as Rocky Maivia. Because of this, he was labeled a baby face, or face. In wrestling terms, a baby face is a good guy, a wrestler with a clean image who is typically on the fans' good side. In fact, fans generally cheer for the good guys—but not in Rocky Maivia's case. Not only did the fans not cheer him, they actually jeered him and threw verbal insults as he walked down the aisle and entered the ring for his matches.

Despite the mostly unexpected fan reaction, though, Johnson stayed with the role of baby face throughout the rest of his first season with the WWF, ignoring the taunts and smiling as he approached wrestling rings in the United States, Europe, and the Middle East. He also kept his head down and mostly stayed to himself during the long traveling time. Few other wrestlers on the tours knew him very well, and he really did not know any of them. One exception was Bret Hart, who, like his brother Owen, befriended the young wrestler, a kindness Johnson never forgot.

Sharpening the Angles

As he wrestled in different parts of the country, Johnson became involved in angles, which are carefully staged and planned fictional storylines played out in the ring. Some angles involve single matches; others, however, are played out over several years. Angles are played as long as the storyline and the wrestlers involved are popular with the fans. The success of the angle is based on the strength of fan response.

As Johnson knew when he entered the business, although wrestlers are highly trained athletes engaging in a potentially dangerous sport, wrestling is still entertainment—acting, with a lot of very physical stage prowess. As in other forms of entertainment, it is all about the show and showmanship, selling the angle. Just like actors in stage plays, wrestlers follow cues. These cues let the wrestlers know what is supposed to happen next during the match. By following the cues, wrestlers can make their battles in the ring look real and sell the match to the fans. The cues also lessen the possibility of being injured. Like a play in rehearsal, wrestlers will work before a match to plan their spots—moves designed to get a certain type of reaction from the fans. Sometimes a spot does not work as planned. This is called a blown spot. A highspot can be either a top-rope move or a series of moves that appear to be particularly dangerous and generally draw a "pop," or a big response, from the fans.

A no-show can also be part of an angle. A no-show is a wrestler not showing up for a match. No-shows are typically staged as part of a storyline. Very seldom do wrestlers do an unscripted no-show because this can result in being fined or fired.

Johnson followed the rules and played by the numbers. He was a good guy both inside and outside of the ring. WWF officials told him to keep smiling and acting like he was glad to be there, so no matter how hard it was to keep smiling while half of the fans in the arenas were hurling insults, that was exactly what he did—for as long as he could.

In the spring of 1997, Johnson's parents and his girlfriend Dany came to Chicago, Illinois, to watch him in a match. Rocky Maivia was defending his Intercontinental title against a heel character called the Sultan. Rocky Maivia successfully defended his title, beating the Sultan. Despite this, though, the jeers and insults continued as he left the ring. Neither

Johnson, his family, nor Dany could understand the crowd's reaction. The spectators shouted that they wanted Rocky to die and worse. Not content to just shout insults, the fans even began making insulting signs and holding them up during the matches.

Johnson reached the point where he could no longer ignore the jeering and insults. He continued to do his job in the ring and do it well, but he stopped smiling. Finally, something happened that gave Johnson the opportunity to take some downtime and to change Rocky Maivia's personality for good.

Time Off and Big Changes

Two important events occurred for Johnson in the spring of 1997. First, Owen Hart won Rocky Maivia's Intercontinental Championship title. Second, in a match with Mankind, Johnson suffered a knee injury that forced him to take some time away from the wrestling business. To recover properly, Johnson would have to stay out of the ring for at least two months. Johnson put this time to good use. He and Dany had already become engaged, so they planned to have their wedding during his recovery time.

By now, Johnson had earned a name in the wrestling business, but Dany's parents were not particularly impressed. Although he was successful, he was still just a wrestler. They knew wrestlers spent a lot of time on the road and that an injury could end his career. Because of this and other issues, they were resistant to the idea of their daughter marrying him. However, they knew the couple was determined to be married, so they put aside their personal differences to help the pair plan a unique wedding celebration, a family event that would honor Dany's Cuban background as well as Johnson's Samoan culture.

Dany Garcia and Dwayne Johnson were married in an outdoor ceremony on May 3, 1997, the day after Johnson's 25th birthday. The bride wore a traditional white gown with a flowing train and carried a cascading bouquet of

Johnson's first major wrestling injury came in a match against Mankind, a character played by Mick Foley (shown here).

flowers. The groom wore a black tuxedo. With his best man Tonga 'Uli'uli Fifita, the wrestler known as Haku, standing by, the couple said their vows beneath an arch of flowers.

After the ceremony, wedding guests were entertained by a Polynesian band and dancers. Johnson's mother even performed a traditional Samoan wedding dance, and the wedding banquet was similar to a Hawaiian luau. In another departure from traditional receptions, in addition to a wedding cake, the guests were served chocolate chip cookies, one of the groom's favorite treats. The number of guests was larger than the couple first expected. In fact, as a sign of respect, many of

Dwayne Johnson and Dany Garcia decided to get married after Johnson's wrestling career took off.

Johnson's Samoan relatives traveled great distances to witness his marriage and take part in the celebration. Garcia's and Johnson's parents finally met for the first time at the wedding. This could have been a tense time, but everyone put aside their personal opinions to support Johnson and his new bride on their day. If the ice was not completely broken between Johnson's and Garcia's families, it had at least begun to thaw.

Johnson was happy to have Dany as his wife, and even though it was a happy moment in his life and one he had wanted for a long time, marriage was still a major change for him. However, this was not the only way his life was changing at this time. Johnson was preparing to make a big change in his career as well.

Chapter **Three**

Turning Heel

In his return to the ring after his knee injury, Rocky Maivia's personality changed. Johnson did not want to go back to work as a baby face. Fortunately, the WWF officials were in total agreement with him about making the change from baby face to heel, or "bad guy" character. In fact, once he was recovered from his injury and ready to go back to work, they asked him to join the Nation of Domination. The Nation, as it was called, was a "stable," or group of wrestlers who share some common element. The Nation was composed of a group of heels and was led by Ron Simmons, known in the ring as Faarooq. Other members of the Nation at that time were D'Lo Brown and Kama Mustafa.

From Good to Bad

Johnson's first appearance as a heel took place in Jackson, Mississippi, in August 1997. After an absence of more than two months, Rocky Maivia rocked wrestling fans when he made his official debut as a bad guy. Faarooq was pinned by the wrestler Chainz. Maivia jumped into the ring on a "run-in." A run-in is a wrestler who is not actively participating in a match jumping into the ring to come to the aid of one of the other wrestlers.

The fans expected Maivia to play his usual baby face role by helping Chainz, who was also a good guy. They were shocked when he came to Faarooq's aid instead and choke-slammed Chainz. Although he was already committed to them privately, this was Rocky Maivia's public uniting with the Nation. Rocky Maivia was thoroughly and loudly booed by the fans. The noise level was incredible. He had been booed and jeered before, but this was different. The fans were showing enthusiasm for Rocky Maivia like they had never shown it before.

Johnson had been waiting for this kind of fan response for his ring character for a long time. In the wrestling business, this is called a push, something that causes a wrestler to gain in popularity. In this case, Rocky Maivia had become a wrestler the fans loved to hate.

However, Johnson had one concern about being part of the Nation. At this time, the Nation of Domination was composed almost entirely of African American wrestlers. At first, Johnson was worried that joining the Nation would make him appear to be aligned only with people of a certain race, and that was the last thing he wanted wrestling fans to think of him. Young people watched the matches and, even though he had turned heel, Rocky Maivia was still a role model. He intended to set the record straight immediately. He wanted his fans to know exactly why he had chosen to join the Nation and that it had nothing to do with the color of anyone's skin.

"Joining the Nation wasn't a black thing," Johnson said. "It wasn't a white thing. It was a respect thing. And one way or another, from now on, Rocky Maivia is going to get respect … by any means necessary."[9]

As a bad guy, this reborn version of Rocky Maivia had a lot to say. In fact, he was so outspoken it was sometimes hard to get him to stop talking. When his fans booed and jeered at him during matches, he jeered right back at them, often grabbing the microphone from the announcer and hurling insults of his own from the ring. Sometimes he called them a bunch of jabronis—slang for "nobodies." He even insulted fans during pre-recorded promotion spots. Surprisingly, the fans loved it. They went for the new Rocky Maivia in a big way.

Another Name Change

Changing from Rocky Maivia to The Rock was part of a story-line, an angle for his character. With each new match, Rocky Maivia gained confidence and also brashness. He went from being a smiling, polite, mild-mannered baby face to a swaggering, in-your-face heel, and it was working very well for him. The fans were responding to this rude, arrogant character with a great deal of enthusiasm.

According to the angle, Maivia was involved in a long-standing feud with the equally brash and mouthy Stone Cold Steve Austin. The feud was all for the public, though; privately Johnson and Austin got along very well. In fact, Austin made statements to the effect that he and Johnson actually brought out the best in each other in the ring.

According to the angle, the two were taking their feud into the ring, a challenge for Austin's Intercontinental Championship belt. Rocky Maivia's public challenge made WWF wrestling history. It changed his name. "Stone Cold Steve Austin, I'm challenging you for the Intercontinental Championship," Johnson taunted, "And if you do accept my challenge, then your bottom line will say: 'Stone Cold—has-been. Compliments of ... The Rock!'"[10]

The Rivalry

This statement started a wildfire of words and insults between The Rock and Austin, which increased in intensity in the weeks leading up to the match. This was good for Johnson because interest in The Rock also ramped up considerably as the well-publicized feud with Austin progressed toward the big grudge match, the challenge for Austin's championship belt. By the time of the actual match, in December 1997, Johnson's

An early feud with Stone Cold Steve Austin helped The Rock complete his "heel turn."

alter ego had pretty much achieved superstar status, and The Rock had become a household name among wrestling fans. The match, a pay-per-view event, was held on December 7 in Springfield, Massachusetts. Whatever the fans were expecting when they crowded into the stadium for the event, it certainly was not what they witnessed. Since Austin was a heel, too,

Disbanding of the
Nation of Domination

The Nation of Domination was a heel stable in the WWF for two years—from November 1996 to November 1998. Loosely based on the Black Panther Party and the Nation of Islam, the group was originally led by Faarooq. Members of the Nation during its lifetime included J. C. Ice, Wolfie D, Crush, D'Lo Brown, Savio Vega, Kama Mustafa, and Ahmed Johnson.

The beginning of the end for the Nation occurred due to an emerging feud between Faarooq and The Rock, who had turned heel and joined the Nation. Ultimately, The Rock succeeded in defeating Faarooq. The personality of the Nation then changed from militant to cool and gimmicky. The Rock's popularity incited jealousy among other members of the Nation, who kicked him out of the Nation. This ultimately led to the disbanding of the Nation.

he fought dirty and won the match. He did this by driving his truck to the ring as though he were trying to run down someone and, among other things, put one of his signature moves, a stunner, on a referee. He also used the move to bring down The Rock.

Austin had the belt, but, according to the angle, McMahon, the owner of the WWF, was furious at the outcome. He said that Austin had used his truck as a weapon and ordered a rematch the next night. Rather than turning over the belt, though, Austin put the stunner on McMahon, and also according to the storyline, he threw the championship belt into a nearby river. McMahon awarded the championship to The Rock as a forfeit. Many fans did not like the way The Rock got the belt, but later in an interview he said,

> *Hey, is it my fault that Austin was afraid to get into the ring with me again? … He gave up the title to me rather than lose it in the ring, which is exactly what would have happened. He knew it, I knew it, everybody knew it. Austin's a coward. He'll come out there with his big truck, or he'll attack The Rock from behind, but when it came to a face-to-face match, he wanted no part of that. Where's his guts?*[11]

Regardless of how he obtained the championship belt, though, the win meant more publicity for The Rock, and as anyone in the wrestling business knows, any publicity is good publicity. Despite his brash character, though, The Rock had a code of behavior. If an opponent beat him fairly, The Rock would admit it publicly, with a few appropriate "wait until next time" statements thrown in so no one would think The Rock was getting soft. Winning or losing, however, was not the issue. It was all about the publicity and the ratings—whatever brought in the fans. The fans were showing up in droves to see what this big-mouth character called The Rock was going to do next. Whatever it was, it was sure to be entertaining. The more fans, the more revenue from tickets and pay-per-view fees

Fans loved the brash, arrogant Rock over the earlier version of Johnson's wrestling persona, a baby-faced good guy.

there would be, which meant more money for the WWF. It was the sort of situation in which everybody in the business won, and one of the biggest winners was The Rock.

Coining Smackdown and Talking Trash

Over time, The Rock became, if anything, even more brash and arrogant. Most people refer to themselves in the first person. The Rock, however, referred to himself in the third person. For instance, if Johnson made a statement about an upcoming match, instead of saying he would win the match, he would say that The Rock would win. However, he would phrase it much more colorfully. In fact, some of The Rock's quotes became part of the wrestling scene. He once said, "The Rock will take you down Know Your Role Boulevard, which is on the corner of Jabroni Drive and check you directly into the Smackdown Hotel."[12]

When making announcements in the ring or giving interviews, The Rock would not simply ask if someone understood him. Instead he would say "Do you smell what The Rock is cooking?"[13] He was big, arrogant, and very vocal. In fact, many said The Rock had a big mouth, yet he

The Rock excited the crowd when doing a signature move that involved lifting his right eyebrow.

also had the size and skill to back up whatever he said.

He fed on the jeers and taunts of wrestling fans. He was getting exactly what he wanted, becoming one of the best-known heels in the business. For The Rock, any attention was good attention. The fans even reacted wildly when he raised his right eyebrow. He called this "The People's Eyebrow."[14] Many of The Rock's catchphrases became lasting parts of the WWE universe. Today, *SmackDown* is its own brand, with a house show that travels the country and airs on television each week.

Meanwhile, in another angle, jealousy was brewing among the Nation over the attention The Rock was getting. In fact, Faarooq, the leader of the Nation, did not like it at all. After all, he was the leader of the Nation, not The Rock. The Rock was only the new guy on the team. Jealousy continued to mount. With two such strong personalities, it was not long before a full-blown power struggle for leadership of the Nation began.

Building the Feud

As usual, The Rock, always the attention-grabber, had something arrogant to say:

> I've got the power because I've got the belt. What's he [Faarooq] got? He has a big mouth, but he doesn't have much else going for him. The Rock is the leader of this group. The Rock is the best Intercontinental champ in history. I've proven myself. The Nation of Domination is mine. The Rock is just better suited to being a leader. If Faarooq really thought about things, he'd realize he's better off taking a lesser role with the Nation.[15]

The feud with Faarooq came to a head during a match between The Rock and Ken Shamrock during WrestleMania 14 on March 29, 1998. Although both wrestlers were heels, The Rock had gone by the rules during the match; Shamrock did not. Shamrock chose to ignore the referees and refused to

Addiction and
Injury in Wrestling

Although the outcomes of most professional wrestling matches are determined in advance, wrestling can still be hard on the health of the performers. Many professional wrestlers are on the road 300 or more days out of the year. If they have downtime due to accidents, they lose money, so some wrestlers work despite painful injuries. Some turn to painkillers. Although painkillers numb the pain, they also make the wrestlers feel tired and slow. Because of this, they take other drugs to speed up their bodies so they can perform. Not only is this mixture of drugs dangerous in the short term, it is also addictive.

Another drug problem that the wrestling industry as well as other professional sports contend with is steroid use. Wrestlers have to have big, strong bodies. They can make their bodies large by gaining a large amount of weight, which can be a danger to their health. Instead, some turn to steroids to bulk up.

break a hold on The Rock when the referees ordered him to stop. When they tried to physically break his hold, Shamrock slammed all the referees to the mat and pinned The Rock, who appeared to have suffered a leg injury. Although Faarooq was ringside, he did nothing to help his teammate who was struggling with Shamrock. Despite his illegal moves, Shamrock thought he had won the match. However, due to his behavior in the ring, the decision was reversed, and The Rock retained his Intercontinental title.

Although he still had his title, The Rock was angry because Faarooq had not helped him in the ring when Shamrock had tried to break his leg. The other members of the Nation were

Another danger of working in such a physical sport is the risk of getting a concussion, which is a traumatic brain injury that is caused by a blow to the head, such as a powerful hit or a fall. Scientific studies have shown that this repetitive brain trauma can lead to a degenerative brain disease called Chronic Traumatic Encephalopathy (CTE). CTE is caused by a buildup of tau protein that spreads throughout the brain and kills brain cells. As a result, patients may have problems with memory and thinking, along with confusion, impaired judgment, impulse-control problems, depression, aggression, and paranoia.

CTE played a role in the case of Chris Benoit, who killed his wife and child and then took his own life on June 24, 2007. The wrestler was part of the Extreme Championship Wrestling (ECW) and performed a signature move of a diving head-butt around 200 times in his 22-year career. This move involved climbing to the top of the ropes and launching himself headfirst into his opponent. The autopsy results of Benoit showed that CTE had spread to all regions of his brain, a deadly consequence of the multiple concussions he had suffered as part of his wrestling career.

angry, as well. They felt Faarooq had betrayed the Nation by not coming to the aid of a teammate. Due to his bad behavior, the team kicked Faarooq out of the Nation. Of course, this began another major feud, leaving The Rock and Faarooq bitter enemies. The new feud brought larger crowds to their supposed grudge matches. One of these matches was the "Unforgiven: In Your House" pay-per-view event in April 1998, when Faarooq, Shamrock, and Steve Blackman defeated Faarooq's former teammates, The Rock, D'Lo Brown, and Mark Henry.

In the fall of 1998, Johnson signed a new contract with the WWF that would earn him a minimum of $400,000 a year. In addition to his new contract, The Rock made another career change. He left the Nation and joined another group, the Corporation, which had been formed by Vince and Shane McMahon in the fall of 1998. Among the Corporation were the Big Boss Man, Sergeant Slaughter, Pat Patterson, and Gerald Brisco. The Rock was billed as the Crown Jewel of the Corporation.

He now referred to himself as "The People's Champion."[16] He had a signature move called the "People's Elbow,"[17] which he used to "lay the smack down,"[18] defeating his opponents. Of course, the name, the character, and the words were all a part of the whole entertainment package. Whether The Rock was winning against Mankind and Ken Shamrock in Breakdown— The Steel Cage Match or losing the Intercontinental title to Triple H, both of which occurred in 1998, The Rock was still a winner because each match increased his popularity. As The Rock's popularity rose, Johnson's income rose, whether from WWF contracts, endorsements, or other opportunities. This all meant money in the bank and financial security for Dwayne and Dany Johnson.

Dealing with Fame

By now Dwayne and Dany were living in a home with closets that were likely larger than some of the apartments Johnson once occupied in Calgary and Memphis. The secondhand SUV was long gone. They no longer needed to be on a tight budget and could pretty much afford whatever they wanted in the way of homes, entertainment, food, clothing, and vacations. This was because not only was Johnson successful as a wrestler, Dany was also a successful businesswoman and a financial planner.

The couple had everything money could buy, but the fame and fortune came at a high price. For instance, Johnson and his wife lost much of their privacy. They could no longer take a walk in the neighborhood, go shopping at the mall, or go out to a movie without being mobbed by fans. While many fans were polite and waited for an appropriate moment to approach Johnson to have their picture taken with The Rock,

Once Dwayne Johnson became more well-known, he and his wife, Dany, lost much of their privacy.

others were rude, pushy, and demanding. In fact, sometimes they would physically push Dany out of their way, shoving themselves between her and her husband. Whatever the behavior of the fans, though, outside the ring, Johnson was unfailingly courteous, thoughtful, and polite, especially with his youngest fans. He knew that many children looked up to The Rock and wanted to be like him. Because of this, one way Johnson put his fame to good use was by always trying to be a good role model. He once spoke of his responsibility to fans:

There's a huge responsibility. It's extremely important to me, outside of the ring, outside of the character, that these kids realize you have to go to school ... get your grades, make sure your grades are up, and do the right thing. It's hard in this day and age to escape the peer pressure. But, believe me, look peer pressure straight in the face and tell those other guys who want you to do drugs or to take pills or take crack or smoke whatever it is, and say, 'Hey, I'm going to do the right thing.' It's just that simple.[19]

Johnson knew that fame had other downsides as well, such as getting self-absorbed and becoming too impressed with one's reputation. Sometimes, whether in wrestling

Despite his brash nature, kids loved The Rock. He has appeared on the Nickelodeon Kids' Choice Awards many times throughout his career.

or any other entertainment field, when people become stars they lose sight of who put them there, and the people who put them there are the fans. Johnson knew firsthand that some big names in the entertainment industry refused to talk to fans, give autographs, or have their pictures taken.

He had also seen colleagues in the wrestling business abuse and misuse the opportunities fame had brought them. Some were involved in public brawls and other out-of-control behavior. Some damaged their minds and bodies with drugs. Alcohol and drug abuse have taken the lives of wrestlers and other sports figures. Johnson chose not to go down that path. He respected his life, his family, his health, and all the opportunities he had been given. He would not waste them.

Another wise move Johnson made was keeping his eyes open for any of the variety of opportunities that came his way. Wrestlers, like other sports figures, earned additional income from product endorsements and appearing on television programs other than sporting events. Sometimes they had cameo roles in television comedies and dramas. Cameos are brief roles with few spoken lines. For some, these cameo roles led to larger parts, both on television and in movies. Johnson carefully considered each opportunity he was offered, and when a good one came along, he took advantage of it. However, it was wrestling that had made him rich and famous. For a while longer, it remained his main focus.

Witnessing Tragedy

Johnson was not about to drop his wrestling career and jump into an acting career, something he knew little about, but he did consider his options as he continued wrestling. Johnson appreciated all the benefits that came along with the increased popularity of professional wrestling and especially the popularity of his character, The Rock. He had earned his success, though, as well as the friendship of some of his former wrestling idols.

The last months of the 1990s and the first years of the 21st century brought both triumph and tragedy into Johnson's personal and professional life. One of the saddest events in his life occurred on May 23, 1999, in Kansas City, Missouri. The Rock and the other wrestlers were in their dressing rooms, waiting to be called to the ring for their own matches. In the meantime, Johnson's friend and former mentor, Owen Hart, waited high above the crowd in the arena's rafters, ready to perform one of his scene-stealing stunts. According to the plan, he would be lowered from the arena's ceiling and into the ring by a cable to make a grand entrance for his match, a stunt he had performed previously. Some say the cable snapped, but others say he became disconnected from it. Whatever the cause, Hart plunged more than 50 feet (15 m) to his death. Fans and performers alike were stunned and heartbroken by the accident. Hart, the jokester, had been a beloved member of the wrestling community. One teenage onlooker said, "We thought it was a doll at first. We thought they were just playing with us. We were really shocked when we found out that it was no joke."[20]

Having to go into the ring such a short time after Hart was taken away by ambulance was one of the hardest things The Rock and the other wrestlers ever had to do in their wrestling careers, but they did it. In the entertainment industry, it is often said, the show must go on. While wrestling is a sport, it is also entertainment, so, putting aside their personal feelings, the wrestlers took their turns in the ring. However, all storylines and scripts planned for the following night's event were scrapped, and the program was dedicated as a tribute to Hart.

Making Big Changes

Johnson had his share of wins as well as losses the last six months of 1999. He beat Billy Gunn in the SummerSlam in August, and with Mick Foley, won the Tag Team titles from the Undertaker and the Big Show in September. He also won the Armageddon

Unfortunate Wrestler Deaths

Owen Hart's 1999 death resulting from a mishap during a stunt at Kemper Arena in Kansas City, Missouri, occurred before thousands of wrestling fans. Hart was not the only wrestler to die young; however, most wrestlers died outside the ring. A few, such as Frank "Bruiser Brody" Goodish and Dino Bravo, died violently. Goodish was stabbed to death during a fistfight in Puerto Rico in 1988. Bravo was gunned down in his Quebec, Montreal, apartment in 1993.

Other wrestlers died as a result of drug and alcohol abuse, including Crash Holly, Louie Spicolli, and female wrestler Miss Elizabeth.

A number of wrestlers have died as the result of heart attacks. This includes Eddie Guerrero, who succumbed to heart failure in his Minneapolis, Minnesota, hotel room in 2005 at the age of 38. Other heart-related deaths include Road Warrior Hawk, who died from a heart attack at 46; Hercules Hernandez, who suffered a fatal heart attack at 47; Big Boss Man, who died from heart failure at 41; and the British Bulldog, Davey Boy Smith, who died from a heart attack at 39. Experts attribute some of these deaths to long-term steroid use and some to the repeated blunt-force trauma of wrestling matches, while others are due to natural causes, such as family history of heart disease.

match with Mick Foley against the New Age Outlaws on December 12.

However, in addition to wrestling, Johnson had the chance to try several other things. He was involved in writing his

The Rock's first book, his autobiography, came out in 1999.

autobiography, released in 1999, titled *The Rock Says ... The Most Electrifying Man in Sports- Entertainment.* This book ultimately reached number one on the *New York Times* best seller list. He also made his acting debut, both on television and in movies. He had several television roles including one episode of *That '70's Show*, titled "That Wrestling Show," in which he played his father, Rocky Johnson, and one episode of *The Net*, in which he played the character Brody. In March 2000, he guest hosted *Saturday Night Live*, acting in several skits, and he played the Champion in an episode of *Star Trek: Voyager*. He also had a cameo role as a mugger in the motion picture *Longshot*, filmed in 2000.

Johnson's first big movie role, though, was as Mathayus the Scorpion King in *The Mummy Returns*, which was released in 2001. To act in this film, he had to take some time off from his WWF duties. Although he was very happy to have a significant role in a major motion picture, he barely spoke in the role. Even though he only appeared on screen for about 10 minutes in total, fans loved his role. It opened the door for future opportunities in acting, which he soon embraced.

Johnson and his wife, Dany, were expecting their first child when *The Mummy Returns* came out.

The year 2001 was also special for The Rock for another reason. His wife, Dany, gave birth to their daughter, Simone Alexandra, on August 14 in Davie, Florida. Next to his wedding day, Johnson said the birth of his daughter was the most important milestone in his life. Despite The Rock's tough guy image, with his little daughter, Johnson was a softie. In an interview, the wrestler and action-movie star openly admitted he was totally in his daughter's control: "[I'm wrapped around] both of her little fingers! I'll do anything to keep that smile on her face."[21]

Chapter **Four**

From TV to the Silver Screen

O ne of The Rock's most famous catchphrases was "Know your role,"[22] but he soon took that saying to a different level as his acting career took off. His success in *The Mummy Returns* meant he fielded more offers in the movie business, and his wrestling career was at an all-time high. That led to a difficult decision for him to make. Should he walk away from the career he built from nothing and take a chance on a career he might not be good at?

As busy as his schedule was, though, he managed to make it work and honored his many obligations. For instance, in February 2001, he beat Kurt Angle to win the WWF title and defeated Booker T at the SummerSlam in August 2001 to win the WCW title. He won the Tag Team title with Chris Jericho at RAW in October of that year. In early November, he also took back the WCW title he lost to Jericho. However, in December 2001, he once again lost the WCW title to Jericho.

With the direction his life was taking, Johnson had already begun to trim down his wrestling schedule as his contract was being carried out. He began to cut back even more in 2002. As Johnson began to phase out his life as a wrestler, the WWF was going through some changes of its own. On May 6, 2002, the WWF officially changed its name to World Wrestling Entertainment, or WWE. During this year, The Rock had some

The Change to WWE

The World Wrestling Federation announced its name change to World Wrestling Entertainment, Inc., on May 6, 2002. One issue causing the name change was the World Wildlife Fund, which also used the WWF name in its logo. Another reason for the change had to do with the growing diversity of entertainment properties connected with the organization.

Linda McMahon, CEO of WWE and wife of Vince McMahon explained the change: "As World Wrestling Federation Entertainment, we have entertained millions of fans around the United States and around the globe ... Our new name puts the emphasis on the "E" for entertainment, what our company does best. WWE provides us with a global identity that is distinct and unencumbered, which is critical to our U.S. and international growth plans."[1]

1. Quoted in "World Wrestling Federation Entertainment Drops the 'F'!," corporate.wwe.com, May 6, 2002. corporate.wwe.com/news/company-news/2002/05-06-2002.

memorable matches with Jericho, the Undertaker, and Hulk Hogan, whom he beat at WrestleMania 18 in March of that year.

Johnson's second appearance on *Saturday Night Live* (*SNL*) took place the following month. Comedian and actor Ray Romano had originally been scheduled to host the segment but had to back out. Johnson was called on to host a second time, and the event made *SNL* history. Johnson became the first athlete to host the show a second time.

Landing Big Roles

In 2002, Johnson also had his first lead movie role in *The Scorpion King*, the prequel to *The Mummy Returns*, which was released in 2001. In *The Mummy Returns,* Johnson's character had a small role. In *The Scorpion King,* though, Johnson's character, Mathayus, is the lead role. Mathayus, the leader of assassins, is supposed to kill a sorceress who has been using her powers to help the evil Memnon rule most of the world. However, when Mathayus captures the sorceress, he learns that she has not been Memnon's helper; she has been his captive. With the sorceress out of Memnon's clutches, Mathayus is able to rally the leaders of the free tribes and defeat Memnon. The film was financially successful. It grossed $91 million in the United States and $165 million worldwide.

Johnson's next wrestling successes in 2002 were in July, when he defeated both the Undertaker and Kurt Angle to take back the WWE title. However, he lost the title the next month to Brock Lesnar. Wrestling was taking more and more of a back seat to Johnson's acting roles, though. In fact, in 2003, Johnson took part in only a handful of matches. In February, he beat Hulk Hogan in the No Way Out event. His next win was against Steve Austin at WrestleMania 19 on March 30. His winning streak ended, though, when he was defeated by Bill Goldberg on April 27 at Backlash.

In the meantime, Johnson's next movie, *The Rundown,* was released in July 2003. In this film, Johnson played Beck, a repo man who is sent to South America to locate a treasure hunter. Though it had some favorable reviews, the film did not make as much money as *The Scorpion King.* In fact, it grossed just over half as much as the previous film. Despite this, it was another film role to add to his résumé.

The Next Action Star

As Johnson continued to appear in action movies, he started to get comparisons to earlier action stars such as Arnold Schwarzenegger and Sylvester Stallone. In one scene in *The Rundown*, Schwarzenegger even makes a cameo. As he passes by The Rock in a nightclub, he says, "Have a good time," which Roger Ebert said was, "like he's passing the torch. Whether The Rock will rival Schwarzenegger's long run as an action hero is hard to say—but on the basis of 'The Rundown,' he has a good chance."[23] Some critics seemed to be surprised that a wrestler could make such a successful transition into acting and find box office success so quickly. In fact, some of these critics said he was a better actor than some other action stars. It was not such a surprise to Johnson, though, who had used acting skills in the wrestling ring for years.

On March 14, 2004, Johnson entered the ring in WrestleMania 20. In an event billed as the Handicap Match, The Rock and Mick Foley tag-teamed against Ric Flair, Randy Orton, and Batista. The Rock and Foley lost. This was billed as The Rock's last match. It was the end of his wrestling contract, and Johnson was now free to pursue acting without having to split his time with wrestling.

His next movie, *Walking Tall*, was released in April of that same year. *Walking Tall* was a loosely based remake of a 1973 film. In this movie, Johnson played Chris Vaughn, a former member of the U.S. Army Special Forces. Johnson's character returns to his hometown in Washington State after an absence of eight years to take over his family's business, which he finds has been closed down. He discovers drugs and violence have overtaken his once-peaceful hometown, thanks in part to the presence of a crooked gambling casino. Vaughn becomes sheriff and proceeds to clean up his town the hard way, with much violence.

Once again, a number of reviews of Johnson's acting talents were favorable. One reviewer wrote,

One of Johnson's early movie roles was a bodyguard protecting a character played by Vince Vaughn (shown here) in *Be Cool*.

Casting-wise this is by far a one-man show for The Rock. Dwayne Johnson, aka "The Rock," has been called the most entertaining man in sports entertainment, and it shows in this film. Despite my reservations of his film project choices, there is no doubting that this man has a presence. You can't help but root for this guy as he's likable and a total hardcore action star.[24]

Johnson was allowed to flex his other talents in different roles, though. After appearing in several action films in a row, Johnson made a big change in character types to act in *Be Cool*, the sequel to *Get Shorty*. Released March 4, 2005, this was Johnson's first entirely comic role, which came as a big surprise to his action film fans. In the film, Johnson plays a country-western-singing bodyguard. His job is to protect a talent manager played by Vince Vaughn. Johnson received more favorable reviews. He was described as refreshing and witty, with a talent for comedic timing, which brought some of the movie's biggest laughs.

A New Name for a New Role

In a few years' time, Johnson had made the jump from one successful career to another. First, he succeeded as a wrestler on his own, without capitalizing on his father's or his grandfather's careers. He had made a success of the brash, arrogant character that fans loved to hate. He had also proved that he had talents other than those he had demonstrated so often in the ring. Although he was extremely grateful for all he had gained from his wrestling career, he wanted to keep The Rock, the wrestling character, separate from Dwayne Johnson, the actor. To do this, he planned to phase out the very role that had brought him fame and fortune.

With his full-time transition to acting, Johnson felt it was time to drop the nickname, The Rock. The Rock was a role—a character Johnson had played in the ring. The Rock was a character with a personality and attitude separate from that of Dwayne Johnson, and although he was grateful for the success his wrestling persona had brought him, Johnson no longer wanted to be identified with that character.

In fact, fans and some interviewers appear to have more trouble dropping the name than Johnson has. In a 2006 interview, he explained that he wanted to be known by his real name:

From now on please call me Dwayne Johnson. I want to be known as Dwayne Johnson the actor, and not The Rock. I loved The Rock; The Rock was a nickname but what's happened is it's naturally progressed into Dwayne 'The Rock' Johnson. When it becomes just Dwayne Johnson, as it will in the next movie Southland Tales, *that's fine. I never wanted to make that defining statement. It just didn't feel right to me.*[25]

The name change, however, never truly stuck. Fans continued to call him The Rock, and as he bounced back and forth between the movie and wrestling world, he eventually paired both his nickname with his real name: Dwayne "The Rock" Johnson. He also continued to broaden his acting roles, playing less violent, more comedic roles such as quarterback Joe "The King" Kingman

With wrestling thought to be behind him, Johnson focused on making movies in Hollywood, California.

His Family Legacy Grows

In March 2008, Dwayne Johnson's father Rocky Johnson and his grandfather "High Chief" Peter Maivia were inducted into the WWE Hall of Fame. The Rock did the inductions himself, presenting his family with one of the wrestling world's highest honors. This institution has been honoring professional wrestlers since 1993, when it was called the WWF Hall of Fame and inducted its first honoree, Andre the Giant. The well-known wrestler had died earlier that year.

Since its beginning, the induction ceremonies have been held in many locations, such as Omni Inner Harbor International Hotel in Baltimore, Maryland; the Hilton in New York City; Universal Amphitheater in Los Angeles, California; and the Amway Arena in Orlando, Florida. Although the WWE Hall of Fame is at present an event rather than an actual location, WWE executives are looking into acquiring a site so they can bring the wrestling memorabilia out of the warehouses, where they have been stored for years. As of 2018, a site and a construction schedule are still several years in the future.

Johnson never quite left wrestling. He still returns for some major WWE events, ceremonies, and press conferences.

Dwayne Johnson has often been photographed taking his daughter Simone to events.

in the comedy *The Game Plan*. In this film, he plays a hard-living football star who becomes responsible for an eight-year-old daughter, Peyton, he never knew he had. Johnson's character has to change from high-living and all-night partying to seeking out ballet classes, arranging playdates, and reading bedtime stories. In a further shock to Johnson's one-time wrestling fans, his character appears in tights in his daughter's ballet recital. Johnson did not have far to go to research for this role. He just had to draw from his own experiences with his daughter Simone.

The Rock Goes Solo

Quite separate from the loud, brash, confrontational role he played as The Rock, Johnson conducts himself with courtesy and dignity. Nowhere is this more evident than in the way he behaved during his separation and subsequent divorce from his wife Dany Garcia. The pair separated in June 2007 after 10 years of marriage, and their divorce became final in May 2008. According to announcements made through publicists, the two now share custody of their daughter. They decided to put their daughter's feelings and welfare first throughout the difficult process.

Johnson and his ex-wife also behaved amicably and respectfully to each other during this time. They did not indulge in public accusations and insults that sometimes accompany the divorces of famous people. The two have avoided public battles and spiteful behavior. Whatever personal differences they have, they have chosen to keep to themselves. In fact, a number of entertainment reports have remarked that all of Hollywood would do well to follow their example under such circumstances.

The two have maintained a friendly working relationship and continue working together on charity efforts begun during their marriage. Among these are donations to the University of Miami, the Red Cross, and some charitable foundations they personally started. Garcia also serves as The Rock's manager under her multibillion-dollar enterprise, the Garcia Companies.

Giving Back

The Rock and Dany Garcia also founded The Rock Foundation. This organization was developed to improve self-esteem among young people who have terminal illnesses, promote physical fitness, and provide obesity prevention education, including nutritional counseling. The foundation also helps young people in the United States and in other countries develop and achieve educational goals. Founded in 2007, The Rock Foundation has supported such charities as The Rock's Toy Chest, which put toy boxes filled with toys in playrooms at children's hospitals.

The foundation also helps sponsor Project Knapsack, which is a pen pal and school supply partnership between schoolchildren in the United States and children in need from third-world countries. Through this program, students are able to share information about their countries, favorite foods, hobbies, and other issues of interest to them. To do this, students in the United States write letters, which are placed into knapsacks with school supplies. The knapsacks go to students in impoverished countries. Not only will they have supplies they need, they will also have the opportunity to learn about life in another part of the world.

Another of their charitable foundations is Beacon Experience, founded by Dany Garcia. This organization also focuses on the welfare of young people, an issue that has always been important to Johnson and Garcia. The mission of Beacon Experience is to motivate disadvantaged students to stay in school and, beyond

Make-A-Wish Foundation

Many famous people, including wrestler-turned-actor Dwayne Johnson, donate money and time to deserving charities. One charity with which Johnson has been involved is the Make-A-Wish Foundation. The Make-A-Wish Foundation was founded in 1980 and has enriched the lives of children with life-threatening conditions for more than two decades.

The Make-A-Wish Foundation began with the wish of one seven-year-old boy, Christopher James Greicius. Christopher had leukemia. He dreamed of becoming a police officer, but his family knew that day might never come. U.S. Customs officer Tommy Austin was a family friend. He promised young Christopher a ride in a police helicopter. Austin contacted a friend with the Arizona Department of Public Safety, and together they planned a special day for Christopher. They also had a uniform made just for him. Christopher had his special day, but his condition worsened. He died a few days later.

Since then, the Make-A-Wish foundation has grown

that, provide scholarships for them to go to college. The program works by providing volunteers to serve as role models and tutors.

Johnson's concern for children also led him to become a supporter of the Make-A-Wish Foundation, which grants wishes to children with life-threatening health conditions. Johnson has done countless Make-A-Wish visits—from putting a Lamborghini in a child's driveway to take them for a spin to buying video games for other children who want to hang out with The Rock. Children often visit him on movie sets where he gives them private tours.

These are some of the positive ways Johnson chooses to use his celebrity status to benefit others. However, like hard-working

Dwayne Johnson regularly spends time with kids with serious illnesses through the Make-A-Wish Foundation.

to a network of almost 25,000 volunteers, including sponsors, donors, and entire communities. Altogether, the Make-A-Wish Foundation has worked with more than 285,000 ill children between the ages of two-and-a-half and eighteen by granting their special wishes.

people in any profession, Johnson also cherishes his private time and enjoys activities that have nothing to do with wrestling or making movies. For instance, few people know that Johnson is a very good light tackle, saltwater fisherman. He is also a big fan of the music of Elvis Presley. In fact, Johnson can play guitar and sing. He has sung in some of his movies, including *Moana*.

Chapter Five

Bigger Than Ever

If Dwayne Johnson's transformation from popular wrestler to movie star surprised some, his jump to the biggest actor in the world must have been an outright shock. Johnson rocketed to the top of the heap in Hollywood—and the top of the highest-paid actors list—by producing a long string of box office hits.

Making Movies

One movie, *Southland Tales* from Universal Studios, was released late in 2007. Described as both a science-fiction movie and a dark comedy, the story takes place in Los Angeles, California, in an alternate 2008. The United States has undergone some turbulent times. Part of Texas has been wiped out in a nuclear attack, and California is on the brink of environmental and economic collapse. Johnson plays Boxer Santaros, an action film star with amnesia.

Another film, *Get Smart* from Warner Brothers, was released in June 2008. In this film, based on an early television series by the same name, Johnson plays Agent 23, a superstar agent with a government spy agency called CONTROL. Following a plot line similar to the television series, the evil crime syndicate KAOS is threatening to take over the world and must be stopped by CONTROL. In an interview, Johnson said he had a great time making the movie and that it was a great experience working with such funny material as well as costar Steve Carell, who plays the lead character Maxwell Smart. He also said it was sometimes hard to keep a straight face in some of the scenes. Johnson had been a fan of the original series, which he had watched in reruns as a child.

Johnson's responsibilities as a father influence many of his role choices, such as Las Vegas, Nevada, cab driver Jack Bruno in the 2009 comedy-action film *Race to Witch Mountain* by Walt Disney Studios. Bruno is hired to drive orphaned twins to a place of safety. Along the way, he has to thwart the evil billionaire who wants to kidnap the children and exploit their paranormal powers.

Dwayne Johnson was featured in the action-comedy film *Get Smart,* alongside Steve Carell and Anne Hathaway.

Johnson expanded his repertoire and also got into the world of voice acting in 2009, playing the role of Captain Charles T. Baker in the animated film *Planet 51*. In it, Baker accidentally invades the alien home planet of a group of little green men and women. In 2010, Johnson took on three major films, including the hit *Tooth Fairy*, where he plays the title character and very out-of-place tooth fairy.

He reprised his role as an action hero with the movie *Faster*, where he played the main character Driver. In a movie full of car chases, it was a fast-paced role many were familiar with for Johnson. However, he also got to flex his comedy muscles with *The Other Guys*, where he played Christopher Danson, part of a cop duo with Samuel L. Jackson. The movie is a parody of sorts of the genre where Johnson found his place in Hollywood. While he and Jackson's characters were reckless police officers, the movie showed that the true criminals and heroes in the modern world are very different from the ones often seen on TV and in film.

Fast and Furious *Fame*

Johnson's true rise to Hollywood heavyweight came in 2011, when he joined the *Fast and Furious* movie franchise in *Fast Five*. Johnson played Hobbs, a hard-nosed federal agent tasked with tracking down the car racing gang that the franchise had revolved around for the previous four movies. Johnson seamlessly transitioned into the franchise, and he became a regular as the movies continued to gross huge numbers at the box office.

The next year, Johnson joined the sequel to *Journey to the Center of the Earth*. In *Journey 2: The Mysterious Island*, however, Johnson showed a softer side to his personality. Though the undisputed star of the action-adventure film, he also played ukulele and sang "What A Wonderful World" during a campfire scene. It once again showed Johnson transitioning the skills that made him popular in the wrestling world to Hollywood. Back in his WWE days, Johnson was famous for his "Rock Concerts," which featured him in the ring with a guitar, riffing

Honoring Stunt
Men and Women

In April 2007, Johnson hosted the 2007 Taurus World Stunt Awards. This is the entertainment industry's only such program to honor the top stunt professionals. Johnson had also hosted the program in 2005. As an action movie star, Johnson has had many opportunities to watch stunt men and women perform their remarkable feats. He spoke of his admiration for the people in this profession: "I have the utmost respect for the stunt community, which is why I am so happy to be hosting the TWSA for the second time. As actors, we truly appreciate all that they do as they literally put their life on the line for the sake of filmmaking. The stunt community is like family to me and I'm proud to be a part of honoring them."[1]

1. Quoted in "Dwayne 'The Rock' Johnson to Host 2007 Taurus World Stunt Awards," AMCNetworks.com, April 18, 2007. www.amcnetworks.com/press-releases/dwayne-the-rock-johnson-to-host-2007-taurus-world-stunt-awards.

on his enemies while singing lyrics that antagonized his rivals.

The year 2013 was a busy time for Johnson in Hollywood. Not only did he reprise his role as Hobbs in *Fast & Furious 6*, he starred in three original films—*Snitch*, *Pain & Gain*, and *Empire State*. In *Snitch*, Johnson played a father who goes undercover as a Drug Enforcement Administration (DEA) agent to free his son, while in *Pain & Gain*, he played a knucklehead bodybuilder turned hapless criminal. In *Empire State*, he turned the tables on his previous roles and played Detective James Ransome. In each role, he showed a different side of his personality and his range as an actor, effortlessly moving from the quick-witted Hobbs to the dim-witted Paul Doyle from *Pain & Gain* while still managing to steal scenes and audiences' hearts in both roles. While this year brought success into Johnson's life, it also brought sadness, as he lost his friend and co-star Paul Walker, who played the role of Brian O'Connor in six films in the *The Fast and the Furious* franchise. Walker died on November 30, 2013, from a car accident.

In 2014's *Hercules*, Johnson played the title mythical character. That year also featured The Rock making an appearance with the WWE. Johnson, as it turned out, was not done with wrestling just yet.

Back in the Ring

Though it appeared that The Rock ended his WWE career in 2004, Johnson eventually returned to the ring. First, he was a surprise guest host of WrestleMania 27 on April 3, 2011. Fans were thrilled, though shocked, that The Rock had returned to the WWE universe. However, Johnson told *Entertainment Weekly* in 2011 that he had always planned to return to the ring:

> *When I left the business seven years ago, I quietly walked away. I didn't want a big exodus or farewell. I quietly thanked who I needed to thank and I walked away. I wanted to 100 percent commit myself to acting and making movies of different genres. I always knew I'd come back. I just didn't know in what capacity. Nor did I know when.*[26]

His returns to the ring have always created headlines, even if they were minor roles. However, in 2011, he officially came back to wrestle, though in a part-time role. The day after WrestleMania, The Rock agreed he would fight John Cena at WrestleMania 28. His 20-minute promo on that episode of *Monday Night RAW* drew massive cable television numbers: 7.4 million people tuned in just to see his promo.

Suddenly, The Rock was back on the WWE circuit, promoting the match and being his old brash self on the microphone as he brought his signature personality to WWE's *Monday Night*

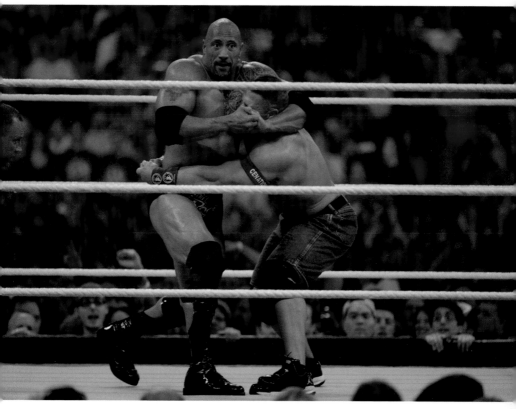

Johnson's return to WWE meant he spent a lot of time promoting his major matches, including those against John Cena.

RAW and other live events. The Rock and Cena even fought together in November of 2011 at Survivor Series, beating The Miz and R-Truth in a match that briefly had them teaming up.

Rock versus Cena

However, the big showdown between the former face of the company and the current face of WWE occurred on April 1, 2012. In it, The Rock beat John Cena at Sun Life Stadium in Miami, Florida, in front of more than 78,000 people. Even though it was not for a title or a belt, the match was the main event of WrestleMania 28, held after the WWE Championship match between CM Punk and Chris Jericho.

Punk won the undercard and the WWE Championship that day, a title that The Rock now chased down over the following months. Though not actually wrestling and only in the WWE stable part-time, The Rock challenged and grew a rivalry with Punk until the two faced off at Royal Rumble 2013 in January of the next year. The Rock won, beating Punk by pinfall and taking the WWE Championship belt on January 27 for the seventh time in his career. He defended his title against Punk less than a month later at WWE Elimination Chamber.

The Rock would once again battle with John Cena at WrestleMania 29 in 2013. This time, at MetLife Stadium in New Jersey, Cena would claim victory and regain the WWE title from The Rock. The match was a triumph for WWE and the two wrestlers. It drew high praise from fans and signaled a passing of the torch of sorts between the two wrestlers. However, it came at a price for Johnson, who was legitimately injured early in the match. Johnson suffered a hernia, torn adductor, and torn abdominal muscle injuries during his WrestleMania 29 match. He wrestled through the injuries, though, and potentially made them worse during the nearly 24-minute match.

Johnson has showed up in the WWE world since that match, though he has not wrestled as often as many fans would like. He is still a huge star in the WWE universe, though, and often appears at WrestleMania and other major events to bring The Rock persona back to delight fans in attendance and those watching on television across the world.

Animation and More Action

Johnson's movie career continued with his now-mainstay role as Hobbs in the *Fast & Furious* franchise in 2015. *Furious 7* was another huge domestic and global success for Johnson, whose films have grossed more than $1 billion a year world-wide. Johnson is now the highest-paid actor in Hollywood, and his roles in 2015 were filled with action and adventure. He saved his movie family and countless others from disaster as a helicopter rescue pilot in *San Andreas* and appeared as himself in the retro reboot of *Jem and the Holograms*. Johnson's return to television also came in 2015 with a starring role in the HBO drama *Ballers*. He played Spencer Strasmore, a sports agent. The show came back for a second season in 2016 and third season in 2017 and further displayed his ability to act in different roles and types of shows and movies. The fourth season of the show is set to premiere in 2018.

The Rock was featured in just two movies in 2016, but it was another hugely successful year for him as an actor. He acted alongside Kevin Hart in the action-comedy *Central Intelligence*, and he did voice acting work in the Disney animated film *Moana*, paying tribute to his heritage as the demigod Maui. *Moana* was an enormous box office success.

Moana was nominated for a Best Animated Feature Film Award at the 2017 Academy Awards—also known as the Oscars—which made it the first film Johnson appeared in to be nominated for an Academy Award. It was also another role where Johnson was allowed to sing. The film's music was arranged by

Johnson's roles have allowed him to act opposite some of the most popular stars in Hollywood, such as Kevin Hart (shown here with Johnson).

Johnson's singing ability has been useful in some of the movies he has made, including *Journey 2* and *Moana*.

Lin-Manuel Miranda.

In 2017, Johnson once again returned as Hobbs in *The Fate of the Furious*, another huge box office success. He also starred as Mitch Buchannon in *Baywatch*, a movie reboot of a television show that was popular in the 1990s. Johnson acted alongside Zac Efron, once again earning praise for his ability to execute comedic roles. In 2017, he also starred in *Jumanji: Welcome to the Jungle*, which was a reboot of the jungle adventure classic from 1995 that starred Robin Williams. He acted alongside Kevin Hart again, as well as Jack Black, and Karen Gillan, who stars in the *Guardians of the Galaxy* films and formerly starred in the popular TV series *Doctor Who*.

Johnson's success at the box office often means sequels, and he reprised roles in 2018 with *Journey 3: From the Earth to the Moon* and *San Andreas 2* as well. His acting career now established, Johnson has the ability to get any role he chooses, as long as the role is suited for a massive, 6-foot-5 (1.95 m) former wrestler.

The Women in His Life

Shortly after his divorce to Dany Garcia became final in 2008, Johnson began dating Lauren Hashian. The period was a rough one in Johnson's life, as he dealt with the failure of his marriage and a state of depression.

"Once I manned up and became accountable for the mess I was in, that's when it all hit me," Johnson told the *Hollywood Reporter* in 2014. "What kind of dad does this make me? What kind of man will I now become? Failing at marriage and as a husband was a heavy thing, and divorce had that special way of knocking me [down]."[27]

In the years since, Johnson has spoken openly about his depression and has become an advocate for mental health in a variety of ways. His relationship with Hashian has endured. In 2015, the couple celebrated the birth of their first child, Jasmine Lia, and on December 11, 2017,

Dwayne Johnson began dating Lauren Hashian after his divorce.

Johnson enjoys making time for his growing family, including his daughter Jasmine (shown here).

the two announced that Hashian was pregnant with another daughter, Johnson's third. Johnson constantly posts photos of his children and has worked hard to make time for his family despite his busy schedule, and he praises the role Hashian has played in improving his life.

"She embraced and loved me at my very worst and lifted me up to be my very best,"[28] Johnson said in 2014.

Johnson presented his first-born daughter Simone Garcia Johnson as the first Golden Globe Ambassador during the 2018 Golden Globe Awards. This newly created role will now be given each year to the offspring of a celebrity. After being named Golden Globe Ambassador, the teenager said it was an honor to be chosen by the Hollywood Foreign Press Association. She said her goal moving forward would be to help young women from disadvantaged communities learn new journalism skills. This particular role is not gender defined, meaning a woman, man, or transgender person can be named Golden Globe Ambassador, which Johnson's daughter was happy to hear, since she is an advocate for inclusivity and equality.

Living Like Dwayne Johnson

By 2017, Johnson was everywhere he could possibly be seen. At 45 years old, he had amassed huge followings on nearly every social media network. Johnson had more than 97 million

President Rock?

In 2016, the race for president came down to a contest between Democratic candidate Hillary Clinton and Republican candidate Donald Trump. Both candidates asked for an endorsement from Johnson, a huge star with a lot of clout among his fans. However, Johnson did not endorse either candidate and explained his reasoning in 2017:

I feel like I'm in a position now where my word carries a lot of weight and influence, which of course is why they want the endorsement. But I also have a tremendous amount of respect for the process and felt like if I did share my political views publicly, a few things would happen—and these are all conversations I have with myself, in the gym at four o'clock in the morning—I felt like it would either (a) make people unhappy with the thought of whatever my political view was. And, also, it might sway an opinion, which I didn't want to do.[1]

Still, politics has been a hot topic for Johnson in the years that followed. He said multiple times that he would not rule out a run for president, especially after Donald Trump won the election in 2016.

1. Quoted in Caity Weaver, "Dwayne Johnson for President!," GQ, May 10, 2017. www.gq.com/story/dwayne-johnson-for-president-cover.

Instagram followers, 58 million Facebook fans, and 12 million followers on Twitter. On social media, fans have seen him praise members of his movie crews, tell stories about the children and other fans he meets on a daily basis, and chronicle his workout plan and eating habits. They also learned that he eats a lot of food and works out in a day more than most people do in a week.

The Rock revealed in 2015 to *Muscle and Fitness* magazine that

Johnson got a star on the Hollywood Walk of Fame in 2017.

he eats seven meals a day. To keep his massive frame, he works out multiple times a day and eats what amounts to 2.3 pounds (1.04 kg) of cod, 12 eggs, and other proteins such as steak and chicken. He also eats two potatoes, some vegetables, rice, and other foods that add up to more than 10 pounds (4.5 kg) of food a day. That's more than 5,000 calories a day.

Writers have tried, and failed, to eat like The Rock, and countless people have tried to follow his impressive workout schedule. The Rock himself represents a kind of lifestyle to attain, and the actor always seems busy doing something. He even released a smartphone app that acted as an alarm clock in 2016, letting fans wake up when he wakes up (4 a.m.) and getting a motivational message from The Rock himself. In addition, the alarm clock does not have a snooze button and has customized ringtones that Johnson created.

An Evolving Entertainer

Johnson has become his own brand in a way, but it is through a positive message that millions of people connect with. Whether they first fell in love with the brash, trash-talking wrestler talking in the third person or the muscle-bound guy playing a tiny string instrument in a movie, they are a dedicated group of fans. He has captivated audiences in a variety of mediums in a way few people ever have in the modern entertainment business.

As the world changes and the ways people entertain themselves evolve, one thing seems clear: Dwayne Johnson will continue to evolve as well. As someone who has changed careers and seemingly excelled at everything he has tried, it is hard to imagine a career change that would be met with anything but success.

Notes

Introduction: Talent and Charisma

1. Quoted in Caity Weaver, "Dwayne Johnson For President!" *GQ*, May 10, 2017. www.gq.com/story/dwayne-johnson-for-president-cover.

Chapter One: Born into the Ring Life

2. Quoted in Dan Ross, *The Story of the Wrestler They Call "The Rock."* Philadelphia, PA: Chelsea House, 2000, p. 17.

3. Quoted in Dwayne "The Rock" Johnson and Joseph Layden, *The Rock Says ... The Most Electrifying Man in Sports-Entertainment.* New York, NY: HarperEntertainment, 1999, p. 45.

4. Quoted in Jacqueline Laks Gorman, *Dwayne "The Rock" Johnson*. New York, NY: Gareth Stevens Publishing, 2008, p. 15.

5. Quoted in "The Game Plan—Dwayne 'The Rock' Johnson Interview," indieLondon, March 5, 2008. www.indielondon.co.uk/Film-Review/the-game-plan-dwayne-the-rock-johnson-interview.

6. Quoted in Chris Serico, "Dwayne 'The Rock' Johnson Shares Inspiring Message for People with Depression," Today.com, November 17, 2015. www.today.com/health/dwayne-rock-johnson-shares-inspiring-message-people-depression-t56586.

Chapter Two: Becoming a Celebrity Wrestler

7. Johnson and Layden, *The Rock Says*, p. 138.

8. Johnson and Layden, *The Rock Says*, pp. 138–139.

Chapter Three: Turning Heel

9. Johnson and Layden, *The Rock Says*, p. 160.

10. Quoted in Johnson and Layden, *The Rock Says*, p. 161.

11. Quoted in Ross, *The Story of the Wrestler*, p. 41.

12. Quoted in Lucas Berndt. "My Top Ten WWE Catchphrases," BleacherReport, May 8, 2009. bleacherreport.com/articles/170899-top-ten-wwe-catchphrases.

13. Quoted in Johnson and Layden, *The Rock Says*, p. 239.

14. Quoted in Johnson and Layden, *The Rock Says*, p. 52.

15. Quoted in Ross, *The Story of the Wrestler*, pp. 42–43.

16. Johnson and Layden, *The Rock Says* p. 182.

17. Johnson and Layden, *The Rock Says*, p. 246.

18. Johnson and Layden, *The Rock Says*, p. 228.

19. Quoted in Ross, *The Story of the Wrestler*, p. 45.

20. Quoted in "Wrestler Owen Hart Killed in Fall During Stunt," CNN.com, May 24, 1999. www.cnn.com/US/9905/24/wrestler.dies.04/index.html.

21. Quoted in "Dwayne Johnson is Whipped by His Daughter," *People*, September 21, 2007. celebritybabies.people.com/2007/09/21/dwayne-johnson-2/.

Chapter Four: From TV to the Silver Screen

22. Quoted in Jesse Weiss, "The Rock Says, 'Know Your Role,'" Sociology In Focus, January 18, 2017. sociologyinfocus.com/2017/01/the-rock-says-know-your-role/.

23. Quoted in Roger Ebert, "The Rundown," RogerEbert.com, September 26, 2003. www.rogerebert.com/reviews/the-rundown.

24. Mark McCloud, "Movie Reviews," Celebritywonder. com. www.celebritywonder.com/movie/2004_Walking_Tall.html.

25. Quoted in WENN, "Johnson: 'Don't Call Me The Rock,'" Contactmusic.com, September 11, 2006. www.contactmusic.com/dwayne-johnson/news/johnson-dont-call-me-the-rock_1007912.

Chapter Five: Bigger Than Ever

26. Quoted in Brad Wete, "Dwayne 'The Rock' Johnson Talks About His Return to the WWE on the Eve of WrestleMania XXVII," *Entertainment Weekly*, March 24, 2011. ew.com/article/2011/03/24/dwayne-johnson-the-rock-wrestlemania-27/.

27. Quoted in Stephen Galloway, "The Drive (and Despair) of The Rock: Dwayne Johnson on His Depression, Decision to Fire Agents and Paul Walker's Death," *The Hollywood Reporter*, July 18, 2014. www.hollywoodreporter.com/features/drive-despair-rock-dwayne-johnson-712689.

28. Quoted in Galloway, "The Drive (and Despair) of The Rock."

Dwayne Johnson Year by Year

1972

On May 2, Dwayne Douglas Johnson is born in Hayward, California.

1991

Johnson begins college and joins the football team at the University of Miami.

1995

Johnson graduates from the University of Miami and briefly plays for the Calgary Stampeders, a franchise in the Canadian Football League.

1996

As Flex Kavana, Johnson's professional wrestling debut with the USWA occurs in Tennessee. In November, he debuts as Rocky Maivia with the WWF at Madison Square Garden in New York City.

1997

Johnson wins first WWF title from Triple H on February 13, loses title to Owen Hart on April 12, marries Dany Garcia on May 3, turns heel and becomes The Rock, and joins Nation of Domination.

1998

Johnson takes over Nation of Domination from Faarooq; in November, he wins WWF World Title in the Survivor Series by beating Mankind; and on December 29 he loses the World Title to Mankind.

1999

The WWF World title passes back and forth between The Rock, Mankind, and Steve Austin; Johnson writes his autobiography *The Rock Says … The Most Electrifying Man in Sports- Entertainment.*

2000

Backlash beats Triple H to take back the WWF title in April; in the King of the Ring six-man tag-team match in June, The Rock, Kane, and the Undertaker win WWF Tag Team title.

2001

The Mummy Returns is released with Johnson playing the Scorpion King; he splits his time between making movies and his wrestling career.

2002

Johnson has lead role in *The Scorpion King*; he begins cutting back on number of wrestling matches; and in July, he beats the Undertaker and Kurt Angle in the Vengeance series to take the WWE title.

2003

The movie *The Rundown* is released in September.

2004

Johnson participates in WrestleMania 20, in March; *Walking Tall* is released in April.

2005

Be Cool is released in March; *Doom* is released in October.

2006

Gridiron Gang is released in September.

2007

Dwayne and Dany Johnson announce their separation; *Southland Tales* is released.

2008

In March, Johnson inducts his father Rocky Johnson and his late grandfather "High Chief" Peter Maivia into the WWE Hall of Fame; the Johnsons' divorce becomes final in May; *Get Smart* is released in June.

2009

Race to Witch Mountain is released; Johnson does voice acting in *Planet 51*.

2010

Tooth Fairy is released in January; *The Other Guys* is released in August; and *Faster* is released in November.

2011

Johnson appears at WrestleMania 27 in April; Johnson agrees to fight John Cena at WrestleMania 28; *Fast Five* is released in April; and Johnson wrestles at Survivor Series in November.

2012

Johnson beats John Cena at WrestleMania 28.

2013

Johnson beats CM Punk to win WWE Championship in January at Royal Rumble; Johnson loses title to Cena at WrestleMania 29; Johnson suffers injury in match and needs surgery; *Pain & Gain* is released in April; and *Fast & Furious 6* is released in May.

2014

Johnson stars in *Hercules* in July.

2015

Johnson stars in *Furious 7* and *San Andreas*; Johnson is featured in the premiere of the HBO series *Ballers* in June.

2016

Johnson stars in *Central Intelligence* in June; Johnson provides the voice for Maui in Disney's *Moana* in November; his daughter Jasmine Lia is born in December.

2017

Johnson stars in *The Fate of the Furious*, *Baywatch*, and *Jumanji: Welcome to the Jungle*.

For More Information

Books

Corrick, James A. *Dwayne "The Rock" Johnson*. Broomall, PA: Mason Crest, 2013.
This biography of Dwayne "The Rock" Johnson covers his childhood, his time as a wrestler, and his acting career.

Jones, Jen. *Dwayne Johnson*. North Mankato, MN: Capstone Press, 2017.
Jones's book explores Johnson's life as an action movie star.

Kjelle, Marylou Morano. *Dwayne "The Rock" Johnson*. Hockessin, DE: Mitchell Lane Publishers, 2009.
This book examines Johnson's wrestling and acting career.

Kortemeier, Todd. *Superstars of WWE*. Mankato, MN: Amicus High Interest, 2017.
This book presents facts about some of the WWE's most well-known wrestlers, such as The Rock, John Cena, and Randy Orton.

Shaffer, Jody Jensen. *Dwayne "The Rock" Johnson*. Mankato, MN: Child's World, 2013.
Details on Johnson's childhood up to his rise to fame as a famous actor are examined in this book.

Websites

Project Rock
(projectrockofficial.com/)
The Rock's official website chronicles the various projects he is
  working on and includes links to follow him on social media.

The Rock on Facebook
(www.facebook.com/DwayneJohnson/)
The website is The Rock's official Facebook page, which he
  updates with his latest projects and videos.

The Rock on Instagram
(www.instagram.com/therock/?hl=en)
The official Instagram page of Dwayne Johnson is a great resource
  to follow his latest workouts, see what movies he is filming,
  and get daily encouragement from The Rock himself.

The Rock on Twitter
(twitter.com/TheRock)
The official Twitter page of Dwayne Johnson includes his upcoming movie trailers, appearances, and other news regarding the
  star's life and career.

World Wrestling Entertainment
(www.wwe.com)
This official website of the WWE includes information on WWE
  stars, pay-per-view schedules, and upcoming events.

Index

Picture Credits

About the Author

Ryan Nagelhout is an author and journalist who specializes in writing about sports. He's written hundreds of books, with topics ranging from baseball superstar David Ortiz and the Apollo 11 moon landing to digital encryption and decryption. As a journalist, he's covered sports, reviewed restaurants, and written features about the arts. Ryan has a bachelor's degree in Communication Studies from Canisius College in Buffalo, with a minor in Classics. He enjoys spending time with friends playing board games, bouldering, and hiking the Niagara Gorge in his hometown of Niagara Falls, New York.